They Were SINGLE Too

8 BIBLICAL ROLE MODELS

David M. Hoffeditz

Kregel
Publications

They Were Single Too: Eight Biblical Role Models
© 2005 by David M. Hoffeditz

Published by Kregel Publications, a division of Kregel, Inc., P.O. Box 2607, Grand Rapids, MI 49501.

Library of Congress Cataloging-in-Publication Data
Hoffeditz, David M.
 They were single, too: 8 biblical role models / by David M. Hoffeditz.
  p. cm.
 Includes bibliographical references and index.
 1. Single people—Religious life. 2. Single people—Conduct of life. 3. Bible—Biography. I. Title.
BV4596.S5H64 2005   248.8'4—dc22   2005022169

ISBN 0-8254-2776-2

Printed in the United States of America
05 06 07 08 09 / 5 4 3 2 1

Contents

Introduction

Nearly three years ago, I was asked for the first time to speak at a singles conference. The group wanted someone to address the subject of walking with the Lord in the midst of living single. The thought of "being exposed" plagued my mind. I feared that my facade of self-sufficiency would collapse under the stress of speaking at this retreat, as I knew my inward struggles surrounding the whole idea of solo living. I had dedicated my life to the study of the Scriptures, but had personally avoided what God had to say on the issue. I was afraid—afraid that maybe people were right, that being single was not God's first choice, and as a result, I should settle down with someone so I could be "complete." Or worse, maybe the single life was some kind of "gift." If so, then this "gift" resembles the type of Christmas gift you would receive from your Aunt Lilly. You know the kind—an orange and brown crocheted sweater with one sleeve longer than the other.

Preparing for the retreat *forced* me to turn to God's Word. Through examination of the Scriptures, I discovered liberation from several shackles about living the single life—shackles placed on me by others and even by myself. My desire in the chapters that follow is to explore with you what God's Word says about singleness. I have read many books on singleness and have been greatly disappointed. Only a couple of authors wrestle through 1 Corinthians 7, while most deal with how to cope with the "plight," provide an inspirational Kumbaya land, or establish twelve steps for a thriving singles ministry. These are not the goals of this book. I have no desire to throw a pity party, create a dating service, or cast stones at the church. Rather, my purpose in writing centers upon taking a fresh look at exactly what the Scriptures say about singleness. Since there is only one chapter in the Old or New Testament that specifically addresses this topic (1 Cor. 7), we will also explore eight individuals in the Bible who were single at some point in their adult life. In so doing, we will witness not only the blessings of living solo, but also the discouragements, disappointments, and struggles. These eight portraits will capture how God intends for men and women—single or married—to live in this fallen world. Our aim will be to demonstrate, through the lives of these men and women, how one can truly serve God and be single.

This study is not just for the single person. My prayer is that anyone who sincerely desires to know what the Scriptures say on this subject will read this book. Preconceived notions, biases, and cultural "ideals" must give way to God's Word. After all, the single man from Nazareth did say, "The person who has my commandments and obeys them is the one who loves me" (John 14:21).

An endeavor such as this certainly involves numerous people. I especially want to thank Sheré Myers, Jill Zwyghuizen, and Rebecca Cragoe for countless hours of editing and a "feminine" touch. Of course, any errors that remain should be credited to my account. Gratitude also needs to be extended to Jim Weaver with Kregel Publications and to Mark Miller for their encouragement to pen this work. Finally, I am grateful for my parents who, while beautifully modeling the "gift of marriage," provide understanding and encouragement as I live out my "gift of singleness."

1

Paul

The "Gift" of Singleness

> Wherever the single person is, God is doing something. You can't alter it; you can't add something to it; you can't take something from it. God does His work so He can grow that person to be like Himself. Then when others see God in that person, His purpose has been fulfilled.
>
> —Luci Swindoll
> (author, speaker, and never-been-married single)

An airline ticket to San Diego, a box of assorted chocolates, or even a pair of socks could constitute a gift. However, the use of this noun in reference to singleness leaves us wondering if an individual is speaking the correct language; while in English *gift* denotes a present or talent, in German the word *gift* refers to poison or toxin. Even the word *celibacy* raises images of something you might observe in a freak show. And yet, I fear the same dreadful notion carries over when people refer to a man or woman who has "the gift of singleness." After all, the thinking goes, a "normal" person would never choose to live alone. The argument continues with a citing of God's creation of Eve for Adam, demonstrating that one is so much better off married. Consequently, the "gift" is portrayed as a curse rather than a blessing.

The reference to singleness as a "gift" originates in one of Paul's letters to the Corinthians. As a single adult serving Christ, Paul wishes that all men and women could be like him (cf. 1 Cor. 7:7). What exactly is this gift of singleness Paul is referring to in his letter to the believers at Corinth? Is the term used to provide a conciliatory token for losing in some cruel, cosmic Russian roulette game? In this chapter, we will explore Paul's words in 1 Corinthians 7, how these words are evidenced in his own ministry, and how they should be understood for us today.

Two Gifts and Two Questions

Understanding Paul's words begins with noting their context. Paul writes to believers in Corinth to correct erroneous practices, attack false teachers, and provide instruction concerning the offering for poverty-stricken believers in Jerusalem.

Despite several historical and geographical differences, the culture of Corinth bears a strong resemblance to present-day American culture. A prominent Bible scholar, Anthony Thiselton, states that Corinthian culture was "self-sufficient, self-congratulatory . . . coupled with an obsession about peer-group prestige, success in competition, their devaluing of tradition and universals, and near contempt for those without standing in some chosen value system." And as such, "1 Corinthians stands in a distinctive position of relevance to our own times."[1]

While her members possessed many gifts and abilities (such as the spiritual gifts seen in chaps. 12–13; see also 1:4–7), the church in Corinth remained spiritually immature (3:1–4). Resembling her culture, the church's immaturity even included gross sexual sin.[2] For instance, in chapter 5 we read not only of a man sleeping with his stepmother but also of many individuals within the church boasting of allowing it to continue. In response to this perverse culture and to particular believers who embraced such activity, some of the Corinthian believers overreacted and forbade sexual relations even in marriage.[3]

The apostle addresses these extremes of promiscuity and abstinence within the local body of believers, first concentrating on the importance of maintaining sexual activity within the confines of marriage. He then concludes these opening thoughts of chapter 7 by stating, "I wish that everyone was as I am [single]. But each has his own gift from God, one this way, another that" (v. 7). Paul boldly declares both marriage and singleness to be gifts bestowed by God. I am continually amazed at Paul's words. In all my years of attending church, I do not remember anyone referring to the "gift of marriage." Often people neglect to see both as gifts, and in so doing, regard singleness as a social oddity. Finally, note that Paul does not pit the two marital states against each other, but stresses the significance of each gift. Both are given by God.

I am comforted to know that God is the one distributing marriage or singleness. The God who called me before He created this world, the One who knows the number of hairs on my head, and who gave His Son for me is the benefactor of these gifts. It is the Lord who has appointed—not Aunt Lilly, not my mother, not my so-called friends, nor that well-meaning church member.

Yet Paul's statement in verse 7 raises two significant questions. First, how do I know which gift has been divinely selected for me? The common response, even among many Bible scholars, proposes that contentment is the deciding factor. In other words, the gift of singleness equates with one's satisfaction in living solo. Often proponents of this view believe the "gift" is celibacy, and they refer to the eunuchs in Matthew 19:12 for further support of their position:

> For there are some eunuchs who were that way from birth, and some who were made eunuchs by others, and some who became eunuchs for the sake of the kingdom of heaven. The one who is able to accept this should accept it.

As I frequently tell my students, the study of key biblical terms can greatly enhance our understanding of the text. When we investigate the Greek word for "gift," *charisma*, in 1 Corinthians 7:7, we find that Paul never uses this lexical form with an obligation attached. In the twenty occurrences of the word in the New Testament, *charisma* always conveys a divine gift or that which is freely and graciously given by God.[4] The "gift" stands independent of human response. In fact, Scripture never indicates that God's blessings are earned by our contentment. *Charisma* is theocentric, not anthropocentric. Despite periods of loneliness, depression, and need, Paul declares, "Not that

I speak from want; for I have learned to be content in whatever circumstances I am" (Phil. 4:11 NASB; see also 2 Cor. 12:10; 1 Tim. 6:8). We should acknowledge that the immediate context of this verse concerns material possessions and various comforts of life, but certainly we can include his present state of singleness.

Later in 1 Corinthians, we also observe Paul's willingness to become a slave to all men and women for the sake of the gospel (9:19), and we find his reminder that all we do should be for the glory of God (10:31). Because Paul recognized God's many blessings, his focus was not on his marital status but on serving the Lord. In "Singled Out by God for Good," Paige Benton provides a healthy outlook on the single life. Echoing Paul's words in 1 Corinthians 7, she writes:

> I am not single because I am too spiritually unstable to possibly deserve a husband, nor because I am too spiritually mature to possibly need one. I am single because God is so abundantly good to me, because this is his best for me. It is a cosmic impossibility that anything could be better for me right now than being single. The psalmists confirm that I should not want, I shall not want, because no good thing will God withhold from me.[5]

The popular belief that "as soon as you're satisfied with God alone, He'll bring someone special into your life" fails to account for God's sovereignty in His distribution of gifts. The reference to eunuchs in Matthew 19 also fails to support contentment as the key in identification of one's gift, because the context between the two passages is different,[6] and because the word *charisma* is absent in the Matthean passage. And lastly, if contentment is the determining factor for singleness then wouldn't contentment also be the determining factor for keeping the gift of marriage? Certainly nowhere in Scripture does discontentment provide grounds for divorce.

If contentment does not signal the gift of celibacy, how then can I as a single person know which gift I possess? Apart from Paul's statement concerning the lack of self-control (v. 9),[7] the text seems to indicate that the gift equals one's current marital status. The immediate context supports this claim as Paul talks about various marital states and the temporality of them. In verses 17–24 Paul argues that one's social, racial, physical, and religious status are irrelevant. As David Garland writes, "Since all human categories have become null and void in Christ, any attempt to change one's status in order to enhance one's standing with God is to ascribe to it more importance than it merits."[8] In other words, one's marital status directly falls under God's sovereignty and how the Lord has gifted a person. The true issue is not to determine one's gift, but rather to faithfully serve God in whatever position He grants. While neither the gift of marriage nor singleness is permanent, we accept our present marital status as a gift given by God.

I believe we often make God's simple truths too complex. For instance, I frequently discuss with college students the will of God concerning further studies, employment, and even marriage. I find that many individuals are afraid of making the wrong decision and missing God's will for their lives. While I appreciate their sensitivity to the Lord's leading, I do not think God's will resembles Sir Winston Churchill's description of the former Soviet Union—"a riddle wrapped in a mystery inside an enigma."[9] God does not play hide-and-seek with His will, but rather He promises to reveal it (see Ps. 32:8; 73:24; Prov. 3:5–6). A child of God who obeys the Word, establishes convictions born of prayer, listens to the counsel of mature believers, acts on what is known, and accepts what seems incomprehensible will have little problem discerning the will of God.[10] The Lord has a purpose for each believer (see Ps. 37:23; Eph. 2:10; Acts 13:2), and, in fact, He *desires* that we carry out His will more than we *do*. Paul appears to caution the Corinthian believers not to become entangled in confusion as they try to determine the Lord's will surrounding the "gift." The apostle indicates that one's current status is the divine plan.

This leads us to the second question raised by Paul's bold statement in verse 7. If I receive the "gift of singleness," what is the return policy? Is it possible to participate in a gift exchange? While there are days when my independent spirit relishes flying solo, I would be lying if I did not admit that deep down I long to have a wife and raise a family. At times, the recognition that my good and all-knowing heavenly Father has granted me this present state of singleness provides little comfort. As the psalmist, I question how long the Lord will forget me (Ps. 13). Yet, my response should be like the psalmist's in the latter part of that psalm—an expression of trust in God's goodness. In the next section of this chapter we will discuss the uniqueness of this gift, but we must note that the key to singleness (or marriage, for that matter) is obedience. In verse 19 (NASB), the apostle writes, "What matters is the keeping of the commandments of God."

While contentment does not determine one's marital status, satisfaction does bear upon living the single life. Recently I read an article by a single adult who was upset over individuals telling her to be content. She felt this tells hurting singles not to hope or dream, "but to abandon the cry of their hearts."[11] And yet, the word used by Paul for "satisfied," *autarkhs,* was "used to describe the person who through discipline had become independent of external circumstances, and who discovered within himself resources that were more than adequate for any situation that might arise."[12] The context of Philippians 4:11 centers upon Paul's residing in Christ and the resultant joy. Paul's strength, hope, and joy were rooted in Christ—not in life's possessions or relationships. No wonder Paul could declare that he counted all things as loss for Christ (Phil. 3:7–8; Acts 20:24). True contentment—that which is based in Christ—does tell singles to hope, dream, and enjoy life. True contentment soothes the soul, encourages perseverance, and affirms the certainty of the believer's future hope.

The preceding words may call my sanity into question. To be thankful and rest in a frequently painful state seems masochistic. And to resolve that my loneliness is God's gift rings of fatalism. Yet, once again observe the life of Paul. Paul understood what it meant to follow Christ. His declaration "For to me, living is Christ" (Phil. 1:21) stems from a commitment to denying himself and taking up his cross. Philip Yancey, in his profound work *Reaching for the Invisible God*, writes:

> In my own spiritual life, I am trying to remain open to new realities, not blaming God when my expectations go unmet but trusting him to lead me through failures toward renewal and growth. I am also seeking a trust that "the Father knows best" in how this world is run. Reflecting on Old Testament times, I

see that the more overt way in which I want God to act does not achieve the results I might expect. And when God sent his own Son—sinless, non-coercive, full of grace and healing—we killed him. God himself allows what he does not prefer, in order to achieve some greater goal.[13]

Christianity presents itself as an ironic religion. We must give our lives away if we expect to gain them. A response to a survey question "If you are content being single, why?" reads, "Being honest I go through waves of contentedness. I often feel very happy with my life as a single woman, but get stressed about it when I think about my waning fertility and growing older alone. But God sustains me. I am not ecstatic about being single, however, I can honestly say, 'God, thy will be done.'"[14] If we live our lives fully to gratify ourselves, we will miss the blessings that come from God's gifts—yes, even from the gift of singleness.

The Uniqueness of the Gift

What blessings could possibly exist from living solo? Why would Paul encourage believers to remain unmarried? After all, we just observed that both marriage and singleness are gifts from God. This question weighs heavily on single adults in light of the ever-popular evangelical belief that one can best serve the Lord if one is married. In a similar vein, I often hear that one cannot serve as _____ (e.g., pastor, teacher . . . you fill in the blank) unless one is married. I label these predominant beliefs as the "Roman Catholic aversion." Ironically, in the Catholic Church I would be praised for my singleness, while in many Protestant circles I am restricted or disqualified. Surely Paul faced similar statements living in a culture which expected Jewish males to marry before the age of eighteen.[15] While we could debate whether or not Paul was married at some point, the apostle has no problem recommending that one remain single.[16] He writes in 1 Corinthians 7:32–35 (NASB):

But I want you to be free from concern. One who is unmarried is concerned about the things of the Lord, how he may please the Lord; but one who is married is concerned about the things of the world, how he may please his wife, and his interests are divided. The woman who is unmarried, and the virgin, is concerned about the things of the Lord, that she may be holy both in body and spirit; but one who is married is concerned about the things of the world, how she may please her husband. This I say for your own benefit; not to put a restraint upon you, but to promote what is appropriate and to secure undistracted devotion to the Lord.

Freedom from Anxiety

From Paul's pen we can observe two characteristics or benefits that mark the gift of singleness. First, the apostle understands that single adults are free from particular concerns that married individuals face.[17] Before I go any further, I do want to be sensitive to the diversity of circumstances that accompany singleness. Many of the freedoms we will address in this section may not hold true for every single (e.g., single parents). However, *all* singles are free from marriage—a relationship that entails submitting to one another and sacrificing time, energy, and resources. Paul delineates various roles of a husband and a wife elsewhere in his writings (Eph. 5:22–33). Such requirements are irrelevant for the single adult. I do not have to visit the in-laws, attend my spouse's company picnic, worry about forgetting my anniversary, justify my recent purchase, or seek permission to spend an evening with the guys. In a more serious vein, I have the freedom to go on a short-term mission's trip, work a couple of evenings at the office, or enjoy a road trip without the concern of leaving a spouse at home.

We need to keep in mind, especially those of us who are single, that both singleness *and marriage* are gifts. Paul is not implying that if we should marry we cannot please the Lord, but rather we will be desirous to please both the Lord and our spouse. Time, energy, attention, and responsibilities will conflict or compete.

To further stress the value of this freedom, Paul highlights the "present distress" of the Corinthian believers: "I think then that this is good in view of the present distress, that it is good for a man to remain as he is" (1 Cor 7:26 NASB). While the believers may be facing a specific event (e.g., a famine), the context of verses 29–31 indicates a more serious situation—the end times (technically referred to as the eschaton).

In his reflection on 1 Corinthians 7, Will Deming draws a connection between Paul's words in verses 29–31 and both Jewish and Christian apocalyptic literature. He believes that the apostle focuses on the hardships that the world will face in "the period *before* the End."[18] The themes of buying, rejoicing, and mourning found in the immediate context (vv. 30–31) occur in Ezekiel's vision of the end time: "The time has come; the day has arrived! Let not the buyer rejoice, nor the seller mourn" (Ezek. 7:12). And in Luke 17:26–37 Jesus tells his disciples that the Son of Man will come, destroying those who are distracted with marriages, buying, selling, eating, drinking, planting, and building.

The issue for Paul is not chronological but theological: "The redemptive events which took place in the death and resurrection of Christ remain 'decisive': These have 'shortened the time,' leaving believers ignorant of how long they have before the parousia [the coming of Christ] will finally cut short all activity in the world."[19] Thiselton writes, "Such concrete circumstances bring home the crumbling insecurity of a world order which stands under the apocalyptic judgment of the cross."[20] In light of the imminent hour, Paul calls for the loosening of vicelike grips on temporal possessions and relationships. John Calvin in his commentary on 1 Corinthians points out that the apostle calls for "a moderate and disciplined way such as will not hinder or delay us on our journey."[21] Marriage can distract from the truth that we are pilgrims in this world and that our citizenship is of heaven. Singleness creates looser ties with this world and directs our attention to the promises of an immediate future. Lucien Legrand summarizes the issue well:

> Marriage is not condemned. . . . Yet it is discouraged. This is not because it multiplies earthly obligations and petty worries restricting the mental freedom to meditate and contemplate. Neither is it because it proposes objects of affection other than Christ. It is not wife and children which disturb men but their

worldly requirements, real or supposed. The danger
of matrimony is that, by the whole force of circumstances which surround it, it tends to remain a "thing
of this age" and to enfold men in the spirit of this
world.[22]

Allowance for Unhindered Devotion

Paul highlights that the gift of singleness also carries some unique
responsibilities. Several months ago my parents gave me a piano.
My gratitude for this wonderful gift is demonstrated in my care
for the musical instrument. Proper placement of the piano within
the home and regular tuning are necessary responsibilities that accompany such a gift. In the same way, the single life carries certain
responsibilities. The unmarried life is not about self-indulgence but
about selflessness. It is about experiencing the wonderful luxury of
glorifying the Lord in a unique manner. As alluded to above, this
anxiety-free life provides opportunities for many singles to minister
in ways that married folks, especially those with children, are most
likely unable to do. Single adults serve in many of our churches and
parachurch ministries. At the Christian university where I teach,
nearly one-sixth of the faculty and staff are single. My marital
state affords me the liberty to work odd hours, speak at late-night
dorm meetings, attend a Saturday morning soccer match, or drop
my Friday evening plans to join a group of students for dinner. I
thank God for these opportunities to build into my students' lives.
I also thank God for an institution that acknowledges the value of
singleness.

Unfortunately, freedom from particular activities does not always result in increased devotion to the Lord. For some individuals,
the single life means unleashed independence equating to irresponsibility and poor stewardship of their God-given resources. In 2003
it was reported that only one-third of the unmarried population of
the United States attends church services during a typical week.
Fewer than one out of five volunteer to serve in church, attend a Sunday school class, or participate in a small group during an average
week.[23] For other unmarried individuals, the free time afforded by
the single life is spent bemoaning the fact that they are single or is
spent pursuing Mr. or Ms. Right. Interestingly, the theme of anxiety

in the Old Testament is associated with striving for that which lies beyond one's grasp. In contrast to this, Psalm 55:22 reads: "Throw your burden upon the Lord, and he will sustain you. He will never allow the godly to be upended." The gift of singleness is not intended for living a carefree, irresponsible, self-centered life, but for living a life that glorifies God. One of my seminary professors, John Hannah, often said, "We are losing the opportunity of giving our lives away."

We should not miss, however, that Paul never claims the single life to be easy. Study after study shows the number one concern for singles is loneliness. Single adults need to remember that singleness is not an exile to the isle of seclusion. While we will discuss the subject of loneliness later in the book, we can note from Paul's life that necessary steps must be taken in serving the Lord single. The apostle demonstrates in his ministry the importance of people. He identifies approximately thirty-six individuals—married couples and single men and women—who accompany him, pray for him, encourage him, and even serve him.[24] Names such as Timothy, Titus, Luke, Aquila and Priscilla, John Mark, Barnabas, and Phoebe are highlighted in his epistles. In a discussion of what he calls "the Pauline circle," F. F. Bruce writes,

> The evidence for its membership lies plentifully before us in the New Testament, both in Paul's own writings and in the Acts. Paul attracted friends around him as a magnet attracts iron filings. His genius for friendship has been spoken of so often that it has become proverbial—almost a cliché, in fact.[25]

Paul was not a Lone Ranger but rather welcomed and celebrated the role of others in his missionary endeavors (see, e.g., Rom. 16).

A wonderful example of Paul's provisions in the midst of serving the Lord single is his companionship with Timothy of Lystra. In six of Paul's letters Timothy's name appears with Paul in the superscription, and Timothy is the only individual to whom two canonical epistles were addressed. Timothy joined the apostle on both his second and third missionary journeys, residing with Paul in Corinth for eighteen months and serving with him in Ephesus. Later Timothy accompanied Paul on his last voyage to Judea (Acts 20:4) and eventually came to comfort the imprisoned apostle in Rome (2 Tim. 4:6–12). Paul frequently speaks of Timothy's service and their common goal in serving Christ (1 Cor. 4:17; 16:10–11; Phil. 2:19–23). This deep and common bond between Paul and his convert serves as a source of encouragement. One writer aptly comments, "In the loneliness of his dark dungeon, Paul craved to have his devoted and sympathetic young friend with him again. He therefore urged Timothy to come to him speedily, giving diligence 'to come before winter' (2 Tim. 4:9, 21)."[26] This single apostle recognized that companionship prevented the seeds of depression and loneliness from growing (see 2 Cor. 2:13; Phil. 2:19–20; 1 Thess. 3:1; 2 Tim. 4:11).

We also need to remember that marriage is not necessarily a solution for loneliness. In fact, in 1 Corinthians 7, Paul's fullest discussion of matrimony, "nothing is said about marrying to intensify the joy of companionship outside the bedroom or to provide a loving environment for child nurture."[27]

Based upon the above mentioned benefits, many individuals may be surprised to learn that the majority of single adults claim to be content with their present status. The Purposeful Singleness Web site surveyed single adults concerning what they were thankful for, especially as it pertained to their marital situation.[28] Some of the comments included the following:

- "I am thankful for the time I have to spend with God. For depending on God as my help and my refuge."
- "I am thankful that I have learned much about depending on the Lord and the importance of finding my purpose in Him."
- "In this season of singleness, I have grown in my walk with the Father and matured as a person."
- "I am so thankful for being single. It has been almost two years since my divorce and God has drawn me close to Him. I have never known love like God's love."
- "The gift of being single has been such a blessing. The opportunities of this present to minister to many overflows. Ministry opportunities often happen at a moment's notice, and being single allows time to immediately focus on His work instead of our relationships."

Such sentiments can be echoed by many who live solo. Instead of questioning why someone is not married, we should applaud the single adult for carrying out Paul's exhortation and for enjoying the blessings of this divinely appointed gift.

Yet, the question of the value of dating still remains. Is the pursuit of a spouse tolerated in light of the Pauline rhetoric found in 1 Corinthians 7? The apostle appears to leave little room for maneuvering between the two gifts. Either you "burn" with passion so you marry, or you do not, and thus live a life of celibacy. There are a couple of issues to remember. First, Paul's comments are his assessment of the situation, not theological dogma. Repeatedly he stresses that this is his opinion (vv. 7, 25, 40). The apostle seeks only to assist believers in their obedience to the Lord. For instance, in verse 35 Paul declares that what he says is for the readers' own benefit, not to restrict them. The reflexive construction in the Greek highlights the fact that the help is entirely their own. As pointed out by Thiselton, "Paul's motivation and concern are neither purely authoritarian nor largely ascetic, but to maximize the freedom and lack of anxiety experienced by the addressees in the Lord's work."[29] As stated earlier in this chapter, the key to our spiritual success is obedience, regardless of our circumstances.

Secondly, marriage is a gift, not a sin. As singles, we need to remember that God established and blessed marriage. Twice Paul clearly states, "If you marry, you have not sinned" (vv. 28, 36). Those who lack power over their passion should marry, but for others who do not "burn," marriage is still a viable and God-honoring state—free from any sense of sin, failure, or second-class status. While Paul views the marital relationship as a means of preventing sin (*porneia*, 7:2, 5–6), he is not suggesting in verse 9 that marriage is little more than a remedy for a strong sex drive. Rather the apostle seems to suggest that a couple's love may produce such a powerful force that it distracts from everything for the sake of the gospel. Attempting to suppress a God-given aspect of human existence will only frustrate and hinder the believer from any service for the Lord. We would be remiss not to mention, however, that a strong sexual drive is not an excuse for discontentment or the desperate pursuit of a spouse. Purity, self-control, and contentment are to mark the life of a believer.

Thirdly, we need to remember that neither gift is necessarily permanent. Even in the immediate context, Paul addresses those who once had the gift of marriage (vv. 8, 15). Likewise, the gift of singleness does not confine us to a convent. The pursuit of a spouse does require, however, that we acknowledge the difficulties and additional responsibilities associated with marriage. The pursuit must never set precedence over glorifying the Lord or hinder our obedience to Him.

Finally, I would argue we need to ensure that the pursuit does not strip the benefits of our current gift of singleness. If we allow it, the longings for intimacy can eclipse the blessings of living solo. Maintaining this balance is difficult for it requires continual, concentrated effort. We must constantly remind ourselves of the advantages of single living and be involved in ongoing evaluation of our actions and attitudes.

Often, in discussing the "gift of singleness," a single adult will quote to me Psalm 37:4: "Delight yourself in the LORD; and He will give you the desires of your heart" (NASB). This recitation resembles a CIA agent's use of an identity badge. The individual seems to assume that citing this verse will guarantee immediate and full access. The danger with this thinking is great, for it creates a misunderstanding of our relationship to the Lord and can lead to major disappointment. The context of the verse calls for the believer to trust even in the midst of confusion. David writes, "Do not fret because of evildoers. . . . Trust in the LORD and do good" (vv. 1–3 NASB). A few verses later the psalmist calls for the believer to "rest in the LORD and wait patiently for Him"—a theme he will echo three more times in the psalm. The words of this psalm were not intended to serve as a classified barcode. The psalmist would never dream of manipulating God into providing what he thought was best for his life. Instead the psalmist indicates that when trusting and obeying the Lord, our desires will be in tune with His desires. These words reverberate through 1 Corinthians 7. God is the giver of the gifts. He knows us best. We are called to obey Him. As David later declares in Psalm 37:25 (NASB), "I have been young and now I am old, yet I have not seen the righteous forsaken." Delight in Him.

Conclusion

The Lord has allowed all of us to experience a time of singleness. As clearly indicated by Paul, our response to this gift is our decision. Many individuals are ready to take their gift to the local pawn shop or throw it unopened into the closet in hopes that it will be forgotten. Paul's words and life call for two major responses. First, we are admonished to value where God has currently placed us. We need to express gratitude for the gift of singleness. Paul states that living solo is not only an option but also a wonderful opportunity to live for the Lord. Praise God for the blessing He has entrusted to us. We also observed that regardless of our current marital status, we must be obedient. We are called to live holy lives that glorify our Lord. Consequently, we will need to make the necessary provisions. As a single adult, Paul surrounded himself with men and women who could encourage and exhort him to persevere and finish well.

Second, we need to value how God has gifted others. For singles, this means thanking the Lord for the married individuals He has placed in our lives. Personally I struggle at times with jealousy as I observe a young couple enjoying each other's company. It is not always easy to witness couples enjoying that which you long to have. However, when I turn my focus upon Christ, I can rejoice over what God is doing in their lives. On the other hand, married individuals need to thank God for the singles in their lives. Statements such as "What you need is a wife," "Are you dating anyone yet?" or "It's too bad he's not married" fail to take into account the legitimacy of singleness. These comments call into question God's sovereignty and omniscience, and they also lack in love for a brother or sister who may be struggling to serve God in his or her present state. Both married and unmarried adults are serving together as the body of Christ. Each member is important and valued for the way God has gifted him or her.

Paul, an enormously significant individual to the church, lived the single life. Despite the ups and downs of singleness, the apostle affirms this marital status in one of his epistles to the Corinthian church. Both his actions and his words reflect a life lived where God had called him, attempting to serve the Lord in full devotion, undistracted from earthly relationships and obligations.

For Reflection

1. Provide a list of benefits the single life has provided for you this past month. How might you build upon those experiences?
2. In Acts 18:18–22, Romans 16:3, and 2 Timothy 4:19, we read of a married couple who assisted the apostle Paul in ministry. Based upon the lives of Aquila and Priscilla, note particular ways a married couple can assist a single adult in ministry.
3. What aspects of Paul's words in 1 Corinthians 7 do you find difficult? What hinders you from claiming the words of Paul?
4. If you should marry, how will marriage affect your service for Christ? Are you prepared to enter into this union for life?

2

Anna

Left at the Altar

Eternal life comprises everything the heart can yearn after.

—Mary Slessor, 1848–1915
(a single woman known as the "White Queen of Calabar"
and hailed today as one of Scotland's greatest missionaries)

The first time I met her, I would have sworn she was an angel. With her sweet smile, twinkling eyes, and snow white hair, Audrey became a dear friend during my doctoral studies in Scotland. Having rented a room in her home, I witnessed firsthand this seventy-year-old's devotion to the Lord and her love for others. If she was not sharing a cup of tea with the ladies, she was working in a Christian literature distribution center, stuffing envelopes at the church, writing to a missionary, or caring for one of the elderly ladies within the community.

Over a period of time, Audrey began to share her life story, and I was stunned to learn of her past. When both of her parents died at an early age, Audrey and her brother were shuffled among various family members and foster homes. She was eventually separated from her brother and sent to live with a wealthy family. Unfortunately, after several months, the lady of the house decided that she did not want Audrey; so my friend lived with various individuals until her early twenties. A few years passed and Audrey was befriended by Margaret. These two ladies became kindred spirits and joined forces to serve the Lord in overseeing an orphanage. In 1990, Margaret was diagnosed with cancer. Audrey stayed with her until the Lord called Margaret home. Without children or husband, Audrey continues to live alone in Aberdeen.

In many ways, Audrey's life resembles that of an obscure biblical character named Anna; both appear to have missed out on "expected" experiences—a husband and children. Anna makes a short appearance in the account of the circumcision of baby Jesus in the Temple (Luke 2:22–40). Widowed for many years and without children, Anna is noted for her faithful service as a prophetess and for her longing for the redemption of Israel. In this chapter we will examine this short portrait of Anna and determine what ingredients are necessary to produce such an exemplary character.

Faced with Social Inadequacies

Every culture has its own social expectations. For the most part, people living in the midwestern portion of the United States assume that a young man or woman will be married by his or her mid-twenties, have two children by thirty-five, and own a home. First-century Israel was no exception and had its own social code.

Anna fell short of many of the unwritten social codes of her own culture. First, Anna was the wrong gender. In our politically-correct society, we cringe at the androcentric view of first-century Jews. While a few women did obtain prominent positions within Palestine, most women were limited to domestic roles of wife and mother and were viewed as inferior to men. *Ecclesiasticus* or *Sirach*, a book written by a Jewish sage around 180 B.C., declares, "Better is the wickedness of man than a woman who does good; it is woman who brings shame and disgrace."[1] The renowned first-century Alexandrian Jewish philosopher and biblical commentator Philo refers throughout his writings to female traits as examples of weakness.[2] And in a similar vein, the second-temple Jewish writing *The Testaments of the Twelve Patriarchs* pronounces women as evil and the source for most sin, especially sexual temptation.[3] Such negative sentiments were only accentuated in Jewish religious circles. Serving in the temple, Anna would have undoubtedly faced condescending remarks on a regular basis. Her gender placed her on a lower level than her male counterparts in this Greco-Roman world.

While a woman was barred from particular activities and positions in a patriarchal society, she was esteemed for caring for her husband and bearing children. James Jeffers, an authority on the historical background of the New Testament, reflects, "Greco-Roman culture regarded women (with notable exceptions) as incapable of the level of intellectual ability achieved by men. It allotted to women the duty of childbearing and child rearing."[4] Anna's gender-based social stigma was only deepened by her lack of a husband and children. Luke also informs us that Anna remained single after her husband's death. Widows were typically portrayed as poor (Luke 21:2–4; Acts 6:1), oppressed by society (Ps. 94:6; Ezek. 22:7; Mark 12:40), and unable to secure justice (Luke 18:1–5). The absence of children further increased her abandonment and helplessness. In a Jewish culture, a child—especially a son—assured future care and provision for a widow. "Without a legal protector, the position of the widow in Israelite society was precarious; she was often neglected or exploited. Part of the reason for the harsh treatment of widows may have been the common view that widowhood was a reproach from God Himself (Ruth 1:13, 20–21; Isa. 54:5)."[5] Certainly Anna would have been greeted with similar social oppression. Not only did Anna face ostracism for not carrying out her roles in society and the grief of losing a husband and never having children, but she also bore the social blight of widowhood.

In addition to her gender, social pressure, and grief, Anna was old. Luke states that Anna was advanced in years having lived as a widow for eighty-four years (2:36–37).[6] The Greek literally reads, "She was very old in her many days." While we will discuss later in this chapter the uniqueness of her age, there can be no question that Anna would have to address the physical issues that accompany old age. The luxuries of handicap parking, AARP, and Icy Hot were not at her disposal, nor were Social Security and welfare.

While my world stands two thousand years removed from Anna's, her social inadequacies jump from Luke's account and seize me. Much of my life seems to echo hers. The claws of loneliness, lack of intimacy, and the absence of a spouse and children rip deep into my own soul. After all, who wants to appear as a social misfit? Who would not wish for a lifetime partner? According to *Time* magazine, in 2000 approximately 75 percent of single women and 80 percent of single men listed "companionship" as what they miss most about not being married.[7] These sentiments reverberate throughout our culture. The lyrics of the theme song of *Friends*, the popular TV show that revolved around single adults, reflect this survey, declaring, "I'll be there for you." Television series such as *Frasier* show divorced men longing to tie another marital knot, while *Murphy Brown* depicts a single woman having a child to satisfy her longings of motherhood.

My inability to imagine growing old alone and my fear of continuing to face the "third-wheel" syndrome perhaps explain my fascination with Anna and Audrey. Surely they both faced similar struggles and the awkwardness that frequently arises because of one's singleness. Such uneasiness can result from interacting with married adults who are so afraid that they will make some verbal faux pas concerning singleness that their communication resembles Frankenstein attempting to waltz. Or it can result from encounters with individuals who attempt to play Dr. Ruth, making me want to crawl in the nearest hole, hoping that the entire conversation is a nightmare about to end. Even in church I often feel out of place with "family worship" times and the only Sunday school class for my age group—"The Young Married." These cultural inadequacies, whether real or perceived, often weigh heavily upon my heart and I dare say, the hearts of most single adults.

Rising Above Social Inadequacies

What made Anna persevere? How could this aged, childless widow serve the Lord in the midst of all that she encountered? Why do we find this social outcast in the account of Jesus' life? Questions such as these confront us in our first observance of Anna. However, if we look closely at Luke's portrait, we find they do have answers. We observe three distinct aspects of this prophetess's life: a willingness to abide in God's presence, a desire to serve rather than be served, and a commitment to praise the Lord.

Abiding in God's Presence
The first distinct characteristic can be found in Luke's statement: "She

never left the temple" (2:37b). It is surprising to find this marginal-ized character in the heart of Jewish culture. We would expect Anna, at least in earlier years, to have avoided social settings with their hurtful comments and painful situations. Instead, we might have envisioned her joining a dating service or if she did venture into the public, confining her activity to the local synagogue's singles' group. I believe we find Anna in the temple because she had learned to rest in the presence of the Lord.

The question, however, immediately posed is how do we, like Anna, abide in Christ's presence, or in New Testament language, how do we abide in Christ (e.g., 1 John 2:28 NASB)? How do we practice this vague command in our own lives? How did this Jewish widow rest in God's presence in light of her circumstances? And how would resting in the Lord allow Anna to cope with life's difficulties? Surely Anna experienced periods of loneliness and longings for intimacy. Surely Anna dealt with hurtful comments and pining innuendos. And surely Anna longed to have a husband and children.

Anna resided in God's presence because she had acknowledged the Lord as the source of all comfort and strength. Anna recognized what the psalmist declared:

> *Whom have I in heaven but You?*
> *And besides You, I desire nothing on earth.*
> *My flesh and my heart may fail,*
> *But God is the strength of my heart and my portion*
> *forever.*
>
> (*Psalm 73:25–26* NASB)

Like the psalmist, Anna's understanding of who the Lord is and what He provides far outweighed any temporal desire. There will be disappointments, heartaches, and suffering in life. But as stated by the psalmist and undoubtedly echoed in Anna's life, our focus should be upon that which provides peace and comfort not only for the present but also for all eternity. Our relationship with the Lord remains unaffected by divorce or death and is a companionship that is unwavering and unfailing. This elderly Jewish widow's relation-ship with the Lord is where she found true intimacy.

Recently I had the opportunity to gain better insight into what exactly "abiding in Christ" means. I had been invited to a wedding shower. Although any event with the word *wedding* is a potential land mine for singles, out of respect for the couple I mustered enough courage to attend. Having never attended such a social gathering (and never really missing it), I made the mistake of assuming that the affair was a come-and-go-as-you-please reception. When I arrived, I was horrified to find the festivities were already well under way. To make matters worse, I entered as they were playing the newlywed game—just what I needed, couples sharing their life experiences! Struggling even to attend, walking in late, and landing in the midst of a couples' game, I could not wait to make an appropriate exit. As I drove down the road, the tears flowed freely. "Lord," I cried, "why can't I be normal? Will I ever have a wife?" The Lord brought to mind the truths of Psalm 73:25–26. It was as if the Lord was wrapping His loving arms around me as I reflected on who He is and what He was doing.

Resting in the presence of the Lord not only entails acknowledging the Father's provisions but also calls us to recognize the person and work of Christ. The writer of Hebrews encourages us by reflecting on Jesus as our High Priest who intercedes on our behalf and allows us to come boldly before God's throne (7:24–25). Christ's death, burial, and resurrection provide not only the opportunity to have a relationship with the Father but also access to Him during times of need. One reason Jesus can fulfill this role is that He came to earth as a man. This should provide additional comfort to the single adult because Jesus also lived outside the social expectations of His day. While we are never told of how our Savior interacted with others on the subject of singleness, Jesus' world did expect a Jewish male to be married by the age of eighteen. We also know that Jesus was criticized for his social interactions (e.g., friendship with tax collectors and women). What a comfort to read, "For we do not have a high priest incapable of sympathizing with our weaknesses, but one who has been tempted in every way just as we are, yet without sin. Therefore let us confidently approach the throne of grace to receive mercy and find grace whenever we need help" (Heb. 4:15–16). Our Savior ensures access to mercy and grace during life's hardships because He can both sympathize and empathize with us.

Not only does abiding in the Lord consist of acknowledging the

Father as the source of all comfort and strength and tapping into the work of the Son. We also need to rely upon the empowerment and comfort of the Holy Spirit. Jesus promised that He would not leave His followers as orphans but would provide One who would comfort and direct—the Holy Spirit. Jesus tells His disciples in John 14:16–17: "Then I will ask the Father, and he will give you another Advocate to be with you forever—the Spirit of truth, whom the world cannot accept, because it does not see him or know him. But you know him, because he resides with you and will be in you." The Great Comforter knows the deep longings of the heart and communicates those desires to the Father. This same Comforter encourages the believer's heart and provides the strength and peace to continue.

Abiding in Christ does demand a response on our part. We must actively place our trust and confidence in Him. Jesus' position as our High Priest calls for us to come to Him with a desire for holiness, and the Holy Spirit's role demands we stay in tune with Him. When we venture away from the Lord's presence we begin to lose sight of the true source of strength and comfort—a Savior who can empathize and a Spirit who can provide strength. Instead, we begin to waver under the pressures of our culture. I must confess it is not always easy to "abide." At times I feel like Peter attempting to walk across the water on waves that seem unbearable. And yet, like Anna, I must rest and not be restless. As the second verse of "Jesus, I Am Resting, Resting" so gloriously states:

> *Oh, how great Thy loving-kindness, Vaster, broader than the sea!*
> *Oh, how marvelous Thy goodness, Lavished all on me!*
> *Yes, I rest in Thee, Beloved, Know what wealth of grace is Thine,*
> *Know Thy certainty of promise, And have made it mine.*

Seeking to Serve Rather Than Be Served

I dare say that most of us would be content if the story of Anna ended with this elderly widow finding peace and comfort in the presence of the heavenly Father. However, Anna did not confine herself to the local geriatric society but actively pursued ministry opportunities. We read that while Anna was in the temple she served "night and day with fastings and prayers" (Luke 2:37b NASB). Her activity reveals a person totally yielded to godly service (cf. Rom. 12:1; Heb.

12:1–2). Luke further highlights her devotion by identifying Anna as a prophetess. This same title is given to seven other Jewish women in the Bible: Sarah, Miriam, Deborah, Hannah, Abigail, Huldah, and Esther.[8] Each of these women serves as a strategic figure in Jewish history, and Anna is no exception. Anna did not flounder in her twilight years; she remained focused on serving the Lord. Despite her circumstances, Anna endured faithfully.

A Source of Exhortation

Anna's service exhorts us as unmarried adults. She did not allow the loss of a spouse after only a few years of marriage to hurl her into the sea of self-pity. Or if it did, she didn't stay there. Occasionally, I meet a single adult who suffers "paralysis from the past." Events such as a spouse walking out or being left with three children immobilize the individual. Anna demonstrates that the problems of the past must not hinder us from activity in the present. She fulfills the exhortation of 1 Corinthians 7 to serve the Lord in obedience despite life's circumstances.

Not only did Anna avoid the crippling of the past but she also refrained from using the freedoms of the present for self-gratification. In so doing, her work typifies the valuable asset singles, especially widows, are to the church. Perhaps Paul thought of Anna when he penned 1 Timothy 5:3–16. In this epistle to Timothy, Paul stresses the importance of widows as godly role models within the church.

Earlier we mentioned that Anna was well advanced in years. If she had been betrothed at the typical age of thirteen or fourteen, married for seven years, and widowed for eighty-four years, Anna would have been approximately 105 years old. In the apocryphal story of Judith, we meet a heroine who deliberately chooses to remain a widow and dies at the age of 105 (Judith 16:22–23). Judith receives praise for her refusal to remarry and is associated with great piety (8:8; 16:22). This parallel between the two Jewish women does lend credence to the respect devoted widows received.[9] As noted earlier, such respect for widows was largely foreign in a first-century patriarchal society; and yet, these two women display an unusual commitment to the Lord in spite of their circumstances.

Interestingly, Anna's widowhood and her service to the Lord allowed her continual access into the temple. Having sexual relations and bearing children were causes of impurity and would have prevented Anna from social interaction and religious worship for particular periods. Her age would also grant her constant admission into the temple as she would have maintained a continual state of purity after menopause. As aptly stated by Richard Bauckham, "She has been granted the psalmist's desire 'to live in the house of YHWH all the days of my life' (Ps. 27:4) so that she may await the Lord's coming to his temple (Mal. 3:1)."[10]

A Source of Encouragement

Anna's service in the temple also provides encouragement to single adults. The Lord honored her faithfulness as she witnessed firsthand that which for centuries the Jews longed to see—the Messiah. The prominent Lukan scholar I. Howard Marshall writes, "Anna possessed divine insight into things normally hidden from ordinary people, and hence was able to recognize who the child in the temple was and then to proclaim his significance to those who were interested."[11] God allowed Anna's hands—hands which never embraced a child of her own—to touch His only Son.

The names of Anna and her father, Phanuel, also testify of the Lord honoring this prophetess. The Hebrew name *Phanuel* means "the face of God"—a metaphor often used for God's favor (cf. Ps. 80:3, 19; Dan. 9:17). This expression recalls the priestly blessing: "The LORD make his face to shine upon you, and be gracious to you" (Num. 6:25). This blessing was read as a prayer in the first century for the coming of Messiah and His kingdom.[12] Hence, Phanuel's name would evoke the hopes of Jewish restoration to their land. Anna's name, which means "God's grace," was also associated with messianic hope.

Anna's life gloriously contradicts the prevailing notion of how much better one's ministry would be if he or she were married. No one disputes that a spouse can aid in "knocking off the rough edges," keeping his or her mate organized, and assisting in various responsibilities, but as we have already observed in 1 Corinthians 7, singleness is not only a viable option, it is actually promoted in the service of the kingdom. Singleness does not automatically equal immaturity and irresponsibility. Nor does singleness mean incompleteness or unworthiness. Certainly no one would make this assessment of our

Savior's life. The myth that singles are not as effective as married individuals probably arises out of 1 Timothy 3, where Paul states that deacons and elders must be "husbands of one wife" (vv. 2, 12). However, to interpret this as a mandate for marriage fails to account for Paul's words in 1 Corinthians and the apostle's own marital status. A much better understanding of this qualification of an elder and deacon is that it entails a restriction against unfaithful husbands.[13] Paul calls for a leader to behave as a "one-woman man." It is readily apparent that God can and does use singles, as Anna's ministry so perfectly demonstrates.

Anna plays a vital role in the gospel narrative. First, Anna and Simeon serve as witnesses to Jesus' right to the Davidic throne. Since two witnesses were required to confirm one's testimony (Deut. 19:15), the Lord utilizes this social outcast as a validation of Jesus' messianic right. The uniqueness of Anna's testimony becomes most noteworthy when we realize that Jewish law did not consider women qualified to serve as legal witnesses.[14] Second, Anna has a significant part in the gospel story because of her genealogy. According to Luke 2:36, Anna belonged to the tribe of Asher. "Anna is the only Jewish character in the New Testament who is said to belong not to the tribe of Judah, Benjamin, or Levi, but to one of the northern tribes of Israel."[15] At the time of Christ, the tribe of Asher was occupying the borders of Jewish Galilee and Phoenicia—a region rife with Jewish-Gentile friction. The Jews dwelling near this region longed for a Messiah and Anna's involvement would ensure "that the messianic hopes represented include those of the northern tribes and exiles."[16] Thus, not only do Simeon and Anna serve as the required two witnesses of Deuteronomy 19, they represent two key aspects to the eschatological salvation predicted in Isaiah 40–66: Simeon hails the Messiah as a light of the nations radiating from the Jews (Luke 2:31–32), whereas Anna recognizes the Messiah as the promise to the gathering of the Jews to Jerusalem.[17]

There are times when we may believe that our social inadequacies prevent us from serving the Lord. Whether that doubt stems from life's apparent shortcomings or from the rhetoric of others, we need not worry. We are in good company: Moses stuttered; David's armor did not fit; John Mark was rejected by Paul; Abraham was too old; David was too young; Lazarus was dead; Peter was a loud-mouth; and Anna was an elderly widow.

Praising the Lord

The third distinct component of Anna's success resides in her willingness to praise the Lord. Luke closes his brief account of Anna by adding that "at that moment, she came up to them and began to give thanks to God and to speak about the child to all who were waiting for the redemption of Jerusalem" (2:38). How could a lady who had experienced so many difficulties and ongoing social stigmatism have such great adoration for the Lord? How did she maintain a proper perspective?

Heavenly Focus

Anna could praise the Lord because she focused on Him. Notice that the content of her declaration is a direct result of God's activity. The Greek word for "giving of praise" (*anthomologeomai*) occurs only once in the New Testament. The term literally means "offering back praise." The word can also be found in Ezra 3:11 in the Greek translation of the Old Testament, the Septuagint.[18] After laying the foundation of the temple, the Israelites praise and give thanks to the Lord saying, "For he is good; his loving kindness toward Israel is forever." Another occurrence of this word in the Greek Old Testament is Psalm 79:13. Asaph, while in deep sorrow over the invasion of Israel and the plundering of the temple, rests in the character and activity of the Lord. He concludes his cry with the following words: "Then we, your people, the sheep of your pasture, will continually thank you. We will tell coming generations of your praiseworthy acts." In each of these occurrences, individuals are focused upon the Lord and His activity.

Bitterness Blinders

Bitterness could have easily distracted Anna from the Lord. Daily, for years, she witnessed mothers dedicate their newborns to the Lord. Daily she watched women perform their purification rites. Daily she observed God answer prayer requests for a spouse, a child, or both. Assisting these women when she herself was widowed and childless must have been difficult for Anna.

One of the more unpleasant situations I deal with in my office is not academic dishonesty or the breaking of some school rule. It is, rather, when I have to listen to students recount their recent engagements. To admit this petty vice is most embarrassing. Please do not misunderstand me. I am not making light of cheating or the breaking of a school policy, but I find the joyous engagement news leaves me wanting. I am left wondering if I will ever have the joy of asking someone to marry me and remembering the line from *Sleepless in Seattle* that "you are more likely to be killed by a terrorist than to marry after the age of forty." It is in the presence of marital bliss that I must keep my eyes on the Lord. I need to rejoice with those who have been given the gift of marriage and relish in the fact that God has lavished the gift of singleness upon me.

Bitterness will create calluses over our spiritual eyes. Similar to this Jewish prophetess, our focus must be solely on the Lord and His activity. Anna did not run to baby Jesus and ask, "Where were you eighty-some years ago? Why did you allow this to happen to me?" Instead she refrained from asking why and rejoiced in the God who keeps His promises. In his struggle for knowing some answers to life's whys, Chuck Swindoll aptly writes:

> I began to acknowledge that I am not the "answer man" for events in life that don't make logical, human sense. I'm now convinced that even if He did explain His reasons, I would seldom understand. His ways are higher and far more profound than our finite minds can comprehend. So I now accept God's directions, and I live with them as best I can. And frankly, I leave it at that. I've found that such a response not only relieves me, it gives me hope beyond bitterness.[19]

Louis Albert Banks tells of an elderly Christian man, a fine singer, who learned that he had cancer of the tongue requiring surgery. Right before they wheeled him into surgery, the man said to the doctor, "Are you sure I will never sing again?" The surgeon reluctantly shook his head yes. The patient then asked if he could sit up for a moment. "I've had many good times singing the praises of God," he said, "and now you tell me I most likely will never sing again. I have one song that will be my last. It will be of gratitude and praise to God." There in the doctor's presence, the man sang softly the words of Isaac Watts's hymn "I'll Praise My Maker":

> *I'll praise my Maker while I've breath,*
> *And when my voice is lost in death,*
> *Praise shall employ my nobler power;*
> *My days of praise shall ne'er be past,*
> *While life, and thought, and being last,*
> *Or immortality endures.*

Despite living in a world of couples, losing a husband, and being well beyond the point of childbearing, Anna sought to praise the Lord while she had breath.

Conclusion

Nestled in a brief glimpse of Jesus' early childhood we meet what would first appear as a rather insignificant lady. This widow seemingly has little to contribute to society. She serves no husband, bears no children, and is well beyond her productive years. And yet, the Lord in His sovereignty molds and shapes her to serve as a key figure in the life of His Son. This single woman is willing to rest in the Lord, actively serve Him, and mark her life with praise. Ultimately all three characteristics go hand in hand. The one who is truly resting in the Lord will serve the Lord and will rejoice in doing so. Praise the Lord for single women like Anna.

For Reflection

1. What do you think was Anna's largest hurdle in serving the Lord all those years?
2. How can the church better incorporate individuals like Anna into their fellowship?
3. Is there a particular area in your life where you struggle with not fitting the "social mold"? Read Romans 5:1–8; Ephesians 1:3–7; and 1 Peter 2:24, and note what the Lord has done for you. You may want to commit one or all of these passages to memory.

3

Martha

Living Life in the Fast Lane

The liberty of singleness is that single people experience the great joy of being able to devote themselves, with concentration and without distraction, to the work of the Lord.

—John Stott
(minister, author, theologian,
missionary, and lifelong single)

Living in several locations throughout the United States and Europe, I have met some interesting characters. One individual who frequently brings a smile to my face is a widow from Europe. This short, spry lady has a calendar full of activity. If you carry on a conversation with her, which is never brief, she will tell of her numerous responsibilities, "Cooking, cleaning, ironing, mending. . . ." Surely she will asphyxiate herself before she finishes her extensive list of duties.

My friend's hectic schedule is representative of many single adults. In addition to life's daily routines, such as household chores, grocery shopping, paying bills, or mowing the lawn, many singles maintain an active social calendar. In a recent Barna poll, nearly fifty percent of all single adults described their lives as "too busy."[1] Unfortunately, my life could also be categorized as such. In addition to serving as a professor and an assistant pastor, I am busy spending

time with my students. I am uncertain whether it is my fear of saying no, the desire for companionship, or my borderline obsessive-
compulsive behavior, but the calendar on my Palm Pilot contains as
little white space as a piano score of Chopin's "Revolutionary Etude."
Hence I would probably make a better poster child for Ritalin than
author for a chapter on busyness.

Thankfully, we have Scripture to serve as our guide. I cannot
think of a more apropos story than the account of Mary and Martha
in Luke 10. These sisters, along with their brother Lazarus, lived together in a small village called Bethany (also see John 11), and the
three of them befriended another single adult—Jesus of Nazareth.
Their common marital status may explain why Jesus was well ac-
quainted with this family and enjoyed their company so much (John
11:3). Let us look at this account in Luke's gospel.

Setting the Scene

> Now as they went on their way, Jesus entered a
> certain village where a woman named Martha wel-
> comed him as a guest. She had a sister named Mary,
> who sat at the Lord's feet and listened to what he
> said. But Martha was distracted with all the prepara-
> tions she had to make, so she came up to him and
> said, "Lord, don't you care that my sister has left me
> to do all the work alone? Tell her to help me." But the
> Lord answered her, "Martha, Martha, you are wor-
> ried and troubled about many things, but one thing
> is needed. Mary has chosen the best part; it will not
> be taken away from her. (Luke 10:38–42)

As sisters, Martha and Mary may have resembled one another
in appearance, but they certainly possessed different personalities.
While Martha was scurrying around to ensure there were plenty
of chips with the nacho dip and that everyone's glasses were full,
Mary was relaxing and enjoying the presence of Jesus. While Martha
bore the brunt of the responsibilities, Mary appeared irresponsible
and lazy. Anyone with a sibling knows this spells trouble, as Martha

mumbles under her breath, "Who does she think she is? Here I am doing all the work and she's just taking it easy." Unable to contain her frustration, Martha blurts out her complaint to Jesus. Note that Martha does not go to her sister but to the one in authority. Similar to a little child telling Daddy to punish her sibling, Martha asks Jesus to scold Mary. In addition, Martha quickly points out that she *alone* has been doing all the work (10:40).

Martha's response seems natural and warranted. After all, she was entertaining at least a dozen guests, including the Great Teacher. Unless other women were present, Martha was the only one caring for all the food preparations. Mary would have been expected to assist her sister. Furthermore, in a culture that forbade women to receive formal training from a rabbi,[2] it was unacceptable for Mary to sit at the feet of Jesus and to learn from Him. Hence, it is not Martha's but Jesus' response that seems shocking. Instead of pleading with Mary, Jesus praises her. And rather than consoling Martha, He cautions her.

The difficulty of this passage was vividly illustrated to me a couple of years ago when I taught Luke 10 to a group of singles. One student became very angry, stating that she identified with Martha because she was a person who was constantly busy and was frustrated with those who are lazy and incompetent. The student also expressed her frustration at "being used" as a single adult in the church. "After all," she proclaimed, "the church members tell me that since I am single, I have nothing else to do in the evenings." Consequently, the student found Jesus' words to Martha an offensive, personal attack.

Undoubtedly, this story of Martha and Mary does appear at first glance to contain several inconsistencies. There must be more to this scene because Scripture never commends laziness but applauds hard work (see, e.g., Rom. 16:6). In addition, Jewish culture, and more importantly the Word of God, promoted hospitality (Lev. 19:33–34; 1 Tim. 3:2; Titus 1:8). Why would Jesus scold the one who is doing the work to serve Him and His disciples? Furthermore, as aptly put by one of my students, "When Jesus says Mary is doing the most important thing, how does that fit in with fulfilling our responsibilities? It almost seems to me that Mary is neglecting what she should be doing. Wouldn't there be another time at which Mary could sit at the feet of Jesus without leaving all the work to Martha? How do we set this balance in our lives based on what the Bible has to say?"

The Perils of an Overloaded Palm Pilot

Some of life's greatest blessings can also be some of its greatest struggles. Earlier in this book we observed the wonderful freedoms that stem from living solo. As we noted, even Scripture highlights the absence of certain concerns as one of the blessings of the single state. Most singles I know recognize and value these freedoms.

However, there are a couple of land mines that litter this territory. In the next several pages I would like to explore some of these problems in the life of Martha. I believe closer examination of the text will reveal that Jesus' words were warranted. We will note that the activities themselves are not the problem but the manner in which Martha approached them. We will also observe what Martha missed because of her busyness.

The Danger of Distraction

The first of these land mines can be seen clearly in Luke 10. We are told that Martha was distracted with all of her preparations. The Greek word here, *perispaomai*, denotes "to be worried." Interestingly, the word is used only two other times in the Bible. The first occurrence is in reference to Uzzah, who in his concern for the ark of the covenant falling off the cart, reached out and touched it (1 Chron. 13:7–11). What would appear as an innocent and helpful gesture is rewarded with death by God. And yet, as a Kohathite priest, Uzzah knew exactly what his responsibilities were in relationship to the ark (Num. 4:17–20). Kohathites were to carry the ark by long poles—not transport it by a cart. Furthermore, they were prohibited from gazing upon the ark. Consequently Uzzah served as an object lesson, illustrating the gravity of disobedience. Bible teacher R. C. Sproul writes concerning Uzzah,

> He stretched out his hand and placed it squarely on
> the ark, steadying it in place lest it fall to the ground.
> An act of holy heroism? No! It was an act of arro-

gance, a sin of presumption. Uzzah assumed that his
hand was less polluted than the earth.[3]

Uzzah was caught up in the act of doing rather than in honoring the
Doer.

The second occurrence of *perispaomai* appears in Ecclesiastes 3.
Speaking of a time for everything under heaven, Solomon declares in
verses 9–10, "What profit is there to the worker from that in which he
toils? I have seen the task which God has given the sons of men with
which to occupy [or worry] themselves" (NASB). Solomon finds that
the activity of work or life yields no profit. Instead, he continues by
stating, "I know that everything God does will remain forever; there
is nothing to add to it and there is nothing to take from it, for God has
so worked that men should fear Him" (v. 14 NASB). The significance
of life is not in the produce made by hands or the number of appoint-
ments in a day, but in a heart that honors the Lord. The lexical connection between the reference to Uzzah and the words of Ecclesiastes
strongly suggests Martha's problem. Her concern for the activity
stole her focus from the Creator. We will note later that Mary's actions
contrast with Martha's as Mary displays a reverence for Jesus.

Unfortunately, I can relate to Martha and Uzzah, and even to
Solomon's warning. At times my life orbits around various tasks and
responsibilities rather than around the Person for whom they are intended. For instance, one of my duties at my church entails preparing the worship service. Much time and energy is spent throughout
the week arranging the service to support the sermon's theme. However, more often than not, the best-laid plans crumble before my eyes
between 9:00 A.M. and the start of the morning worship hour: the
song leader has laryngitis; an unscheduled soloist appears; a baby
dedication has been inserted in the bulletin; or the bread for communion has vanished. Whatever the case, the circumstances send this
perfectionist into a tailspin. Consequently, more than once I have
found myself losing my patience and becoming far more concerned
with the format of the service than the worship of the Lord. Jesus'
response to Mary clearly indicates that the Lord desires the laborer's
heart more than the labor.

The Danger of a God-Needs-Me Attitude

Another land mine waiting to be detonated centers upon the notion that God needs us. Granted, the Lord wants us to serve Him—and such service glorifies Him—but the danger comes when we believe that our activities will impress God, or at least win His favor. And yet, there is nothing we can do to make the Lord love us more—He already loves us as much as He can. He gave His life for us, loving us even when we were unlovable, dead in sin, and rebellious (Eph. 2). The Lord states that He does not desire more religious activity but a heart devoted to Him (Mic. 6:7–8). Furthermore, we need to remember that it is by His grace that He chooses to use us. We stand before God because of Christ, not because of anything we have done.

The context of Luke 10 makes the above claims very evident. Immediately preceding the interaction of Jesus with Mary and Martha, Luke provides the parable of the good Samaritan (vv. 25–37). The account of Martha and Mary at first appears not to fit here, but I believe the account makes a point by its placement. In verse 25 a lawyer dialogues with Jesus on what is necessary for inheriting eternal life. In responding to Jesus' question, the lawyer quotes Deuteronomy 6 and Leviticus 19:18: "You shall love the Lord your God with all your heart, and with all your soul, and with all your strength, and with all your mind; and your neighbor as yourself" (Luke 10:27 NASB). The parable of the good Samaritan then illustrates the latter portion of the great commandment as a Samaritan assists a stranded Jew, while the account of Martha and Mary illustrates the former portion of the command as Mary demonstrates true devotion to the Lord. The connection between the parable and this scene with the siblings from Bethany can be further substantiated in that both stories would have shocked a first-century native of Palestine. In the case of the parable, everyone knew the Jews' great disdain for the Samaritans and vice versa. The listener would also have been stunned by the lack of assistance provided by the two religious Jews (i.e., the priest and the Levite). And, as stated above, the reader would have been very sympathetic to Martha's plea for Mary's reprimand, and thus would have been surprised by the words of Jesus. Through these two accounts, Jesus illustrates exactly what it means to fulfill Leviticus 19 and Deuteronomy 6.

The God-needs-me attitude also leads to a blurring of the

distinction between the Creator and His creatures. Martha's question, "Lord, do you not care . . . ," presumes upon the Lord. She assumes there are certain things that are important to the Lord, and thus He needs to respond in a particular manner. An activity becomes very dangerous when we allow it to consume so much of our lives that we believe its importance should be understood and appreciated by all—including the Lord.

The Danger of Self-Sufficiency

Not only can we be consumed with the activity, or feeling that God needs our various actions, but also the freedom of singleness can quickly metamorphose into strong independence and then into self-reliance. I learned this lesson during my first term of teaching New Testament Survey at Cedarville University. I half-jokingly tell my close friends and family that this was my time in purgatory. Besides having to prepare a lecture and set of class notes for each class period, I also created Power Point presentations. Add grading, learning over three hundred students' names, and creating quizzes and exams, and you have the perfect formula for an ulcer. However, as time progressed, I became more at ease with my delivery; the lectures and class notes were no longer created ex nihilo; and the Power Point presentations began to resemble those of someone who at least knew how to turn on a computer. Consequently, my call for divine intervention began to wane and self-sufficiency began to take over. My current fear is not running out of material or discovering misspelled words in the Power Point presentation, but teaching without depending upon the Lord.

One of the perils of ministry is becoming so wrapped up in our service for the Lord that we forget we are dependent upon Him. Bible teacher and author Warren Wiersbe rightly states, "The best thing you and I can do is to stop looking at our watches and calendars and simply look by faith into the face of God and let him have his way—in his time."[4] The life of Samson clearly displays the peril of this land mine. In Judges 16, Samson falls in love with Delilah. This woman is guaranteed a large sum of money from the Philistines if she discovers the source of Samson's strength. Twice Samson lies to Delilah; and thus, he is able to defeat his would-be captors. At this point, the average person would have terminated this dating relationship. However, Samson continues to visit Delilah, and eventually he reveals his secret to her—cutting his hair would destroy his strength. Upon shaving his head, Delilah declares that the enemy is present. Samson awakes and declares, "I will do as I did before and shake myself free." Then the writer of Judges provides a startling and sad commentary on Samson's spiritual awareness: "But he did not realize that the LORD had left him" (Judg. 16:20). Samson had failed to root his actions in the Lord. Samson's consistent operation without and in opposition to the Lord resulted in a habit. His habitual behavior impaired his spiritual vision and resulted in a false security in himself. He began to attribute God's gift to his personal strength—depending upon self rather than the Source.

The Danger of Losing Christ's Provisions

The final peril of a life filled with endless activity is the potential loss of Christ's provision. You have to feel sad for Martha. She has been running around in the kitchen, cutting up the fruit, checking the bread, and getting out the fine china, and Jesus tells her that she concerns herself with too much. In the presence of Martha, Jesus further commends Mary because she has chosen that which "will not be taken away from her" (Luke 10:42). In other words, Martha chose activities that were unimportant in comparison to what Mary selected. Jesus' words must have pierced Martha's heart. After devoting all that energy to entertain her guests, Martha probably was offended by such words. If I were Martha, I would have smashed the dishes onto the floor and demanded that Jesus and His disciples order pizza. What exactly did Jesus mean in this response to Martha?

Again, the context of this passage provides us with the answer. Luke tells us that Mary was seated at the Lord's feet, listening to His words. Her posture demonstrates obedience and a willingness to follow. This interpretation is supported by the parable of the wise man and the foolish man. The wise man is one who *hears* the Lord's word and *puts* it into practice (Matt. 7:24). Mary's humbled position also implies worship. In Acts 10:25, Cornelius falls at Peter's feet and worships the apostle. We also observe numerous places in Luke where individuals are found at the feet of Christ (e.g., 7:38; 8:35, 41; 17:16). What "cannot be taken" from Mary are the spiritual and ultimately eternal blessings that come from being devoted to Christ. Her actions show her devotion to and awe of her Master. Mary's focus rested upon the eternal, while Martha's was on the temporal.

Jesus' response to the lawyer earlier in Luke 10 also indicates that which Mary will not forfeit. The lawyer, seeking justification by works, asks, "What shall I do to inherit eternal life?" Jesus's response indicates that the issue is the heart. The Lord's comments to Martha show that she missed the point. Her actions meant nothing if her heart was not in tune with the Lord. It is as if Martha was concerned about the price of coffee filters when she did not have a coffee pot. Until she purchases a coffee machine, the cost of filters is irrelevant. The Samaritan assisted the molested traveler because he possessed a heart that understood and reflected love for one's neighbor. Likewise, Mary comprehended the Great Commandment and demonstrated that truth in her own life.

One of my fears as a pastor is that I have parishioners who are busy serving in the church but lack a deep relationship with the Lord whom they serve. Our service for the Savior should stem from a relationship with Him, not vice versa. Such activity robs our consistent worship of the Lord. Focus upon the present fogs the eternal; Mary's spiritual vision rested beyond the immediate.

Summary

Activity, service, and ministry opportunities are certainly valuable. However, as observed in the life of Martha, these various tasks comprise a potential field of land mines. In the midst of cooking, cleaning, ironing, and mending we must be careful that our devotion to the Lord comes first. The activities and responsibilities of life should be used to glorify Him, not steal from the Lord His glory, create false security in ourselves, or instill the belief that God needs us. Martha missed the joy and wonderful blessing of worshiping at the feet of her Savior. The Lord's presence and His provisions were eclipsed by her concern for the household responsibilities and the lack of her sister's assistance. The second verse of the hymn "Nothing Between" aptly reminds us:

> *Nothing between, like worldly pleasure,*
> *Habits of life though harmless they seem,*

Must not my heart from Him e'er sever,
He is my all; there's nothing between.

Chorus
Nothing between my soul and the Saviour,
So that His blessed face be seen;
Nothing preventing the least of his favor,
Keep the way clear! Let nothing between.[5]

Life Without a Palm Pilot

For nearly five weeks, I could not find my Palm Pilot. I thought my world had come to an end. Names, addresses, birthdates—all lost! Thankfully, my glorified daily planner reappeared . . . right where I had left it!

What would our lives be like if we could erase our Palm Pilots or our pocket calendars? How would we restructure our daily routines? In the above section we addressed the perils of being too busy and the danger of allowing activities to direct our lives. From Luke 10 and the life of Christ we can glean four valuable guidelines for how to nurture a thriving relationship with the Lord.

Avoid the Messianic Complex

Jesus was a public figure whose life could have been consumed with activity. Sick and dying people longed to touch Him, children clamored to be with Him, religious rulers requested one more debate, and individuals sought to obtain "a piece of the action" within His kingdom. And yet, frequently we find Jesus withdrawing from the crowd to a lonely place. Luke 5:15–16 (NASB) states:

> But the news about Him was spreading even farther, and large crowds were gathering to hear Him and to be healed of their sicknesses. But Jesus Himself would often slip away to the wilderness and pray.

This is an amazing statement concerning Christ's ministry. The text reveals that the needs of the people were great and that the crowds sought help from Him. Undoubtedly, death was imminent for some individuals in the crowd. Despite all of these issues, Jesus removed Himself from the urgency of the hour to commune with His Father.

A colleague of mine frequently exhorts me to avoid the "messianic complex," the notion that God needs me to meet everyone's needs. However, we see that even Jesus, *the* Messiah, did not heal every person or minister to every broken heart. One thing that I am slowly learning about ministry is that opportunities to serve will always exist. Furthermore, students and parishioners alike can devour my mental, physical, and even spiritual strength if I allow them. Could Jesus have healed every person present? Yes. But did He? No.

Rest is essential for recharging physical, emotional, and spiritual batteries. This is evident not only in Jesus' life, but also throughout Scripture. The Lord instituted the Sabbath, established the year of Jubilee,[6] and designed the promised land and the temple as places of rest (see 1 Kings 8:56; 2 Chron. 6:41). Furthermore, loss of rest in the Old and New Testament was associated with divine retribution. Micah 2:10 (NASB) declares, "Arise and go, for this is no place of rest because of the uncleanness that brings on destruction." Hebrews 3–4 also speaks of the absence of rest for the unrighteous (also see Rev. 14:11–13). Rest from one's hectic schedule is essential. Even the busy missionary Paul found time for refreshment. A bachelor through forty years in the pastorate, William Still writes, "The fundamental need of humanity is rest, in the sense that man submits himself to God in order that the divine life may be poured progressively into every part of his being. This is negative as far as it requires man to cease from himself in order that the Almighty may fill him with life-giving grace, but it is replete with the positive and vibrant blessings of God, even to the highest heaven and to all eternity."[7]

We must be proactive in finding times of rest in our hectic lives. Medical doctor and speaker Richard A. Swenson has written much on creating margins for our overloaded lives. In *The Overload Syndrome* he provides several prescriptions for averting work overload[8]:

- ask the "how much work is enough" question
- rethink the work ethic
- avoid the extremes of work avoidance and workaholism
- define yourself in terms other than work
- take personal responsibility

- be cautious of promotions
- defend boundaries
- be realistic about the workload
- balance life with work
- develop interests outside the work
- place priority on the family
- keep work work and home home
- consider working fewer hours
- consider a job change
- cut down the commute
- open a home office
- increase work flexibility with simplicity.

These are just a few ways we can create space for a "deserted place" (Luke 4:42) in our lives. Dr. Swenson's words echo a wise man from hundreds of years ago: "Every now and then go away, have a little relaxation, for when you come back to your work your judgment will be surer, since to remain constantly at work will cause you to lose power of judgment. . . . Go some distance away because then the work appears smaller, and more of it can be taken in at a glance, and lack of harmony or proportion is more readily seen."[9] These are the words of Leonardo da Vinci, and no idler he, excelling as a painter, sculptor, poet, architect, engineer, city planner, scientist, inventor, anatomist, military genius, and philosopher.

Seek Regular Time Alone with the Lord

As we observed in the life of Martha, life's hectic schedule can deplete our time with the Lord. I find that when I am burning the candle at both ends, my devotional life takes the greatest hit. William Wilberforce, Christian statesman of Great Britain in the late eighteenth and early nineteenth centuries, noted the importance of quiet time in his own life: "I must secure more time for private devotions. I have been living far too public for me. The shortening of private devotions starves the soul. It grows lean and faint."[10]

Another principle from Christ's life is that our times of resting also need to be spent in communion with the Lord. Jesus took frequent breaks for prayer. Luke 6:12 demonstrates that prayer played a crucial role in Jesus' life. In fact, nine times Luke mentions Jesus praying, and each of these incidents marks a crucial moment in his ministry.[11] If the Son of God valued regular time with the Lord, how much more should we?

Constantly Evaluate Your Mission

Another principle gleaned from "rest" in the life and words of Jesus is that we must constantly evaluate our mission. Martha allowed the responsibilities and duties of life to overtake her. Luke 12:25, 31, and 34 read, "And which of you by worrying can add an hour to his life? . . . Pursue his kingdom, and these things will be given to you as well. . . . For where your treasure is, there your heart will be also." As exemplified by Mary, our eyes need to be on the Lord. Remember Paul's teachings in 1 Corinthians 7—glorifying God must take precedence over any relationship or responsibility. In fact it is through these personal interactions and activities that the Lord should be honored. As stated above, the Great Commandment provided the impetus for including the account of Mary and Martha. "Love the Lord your God with all your heart, with all your soul, with all your strength, and with all your mind" (Luke 10:27). This command was regarded as the heart of Jewish faith—the fulcrum of Judaism was a love for God that consumed the entire person. Jesus did not defend righteousness by works, but a life in total allegiance to the heavenly Father.

Place Your Confidence in the Lord

Closely aligned with the above principle is the wonderful promise that we can place all of our concerns at His feet. Like Mary we need to bask in His presence, listen to His voice, and rest at the feet of our Savior. The numerous responsibilities that stemmed from the dinner distracted Martha. Her perspective was skewed as she lost sight of who was in her midst. Martha's comments are almost humorous. She was concerned about feeding less than two dozen, whereas Jesus had fed five thousand men at one time! Martha was fretting over the chaos in the kitchen, when Jesus had calmed the turbulent Galilean storm. She had no reason to worry—the God of the universe was reclining in her living room. Unfortunately, her outlook depended upon her own abilities and talents. This is shaky ground—no matter who you are.

In 1 Peter 5:6–7, Peter addresses casting our cares upon the Lord. On closer examination of Peter's words, we find that the "casting" in verse 7 allows us to accomplish the command of verse 6—"Humble yourselves therefore under the mighty hand of God, so that he may exalt you in due time" (NRSV). The "casting" indicates *how* we humble ourselves before the Lord.[12] Mary had learned this lesson and was exalted by Jesus. Martha, on the other hand, was attempting to control the situation—resulting in great anxiety. We have the privilege of allowing Christ to take our burdens when we grant Him control of our lives. This humility of "resting" recognizes and regularly admits that this world—and our lives—are dependent on the Lord, not us. The burden of our limitations or the unrealistic view of ourselves and our contributions will fade when we "rest" in Him.

Conclusion

We must not miss the context of this passage. Martha's actions distracted her from worshiping the Lord. Jesus never stated her actions were wrong, but pointed out her wrong attitude. Neither did He excuse Mary from responsibilities within the home. Is the activity of our own lives drawing us toward the Lord or away from worshiping Him? Is the manner in which we conduct our lives an act of worship to Him?

As modeled in the life of our Savior, we need to rest in His presence. In our busy schedules this will demand a concerted effort—regular, scheduled quiet times with the Lord, periods of rest throughout the week and year, etc. There will also be times for ministry, but our souls must be in tune with the Lord. Because of the constraints of life, we must constantly evaluate our mission. Are our responsibilities and activities drawing us away from the Lord? Have we become so busy that we are forgetting why we do what we do? Finally, in the midst of an overloaded Palm Pilot, we need to remember to place our confidence in Him. Allow the Lord to have our anxious thoughts and concerns as we humble ourselves before Him.

For Reflection

1. Assess your weekly calendar. Are your activities drawing you closer to God or are you missing your quiet times with the Lord because of your numerous activities?

2. Identify one or two ways in which you can break away for a period of rest in this next week. Be specific (e.g., spend an evening at home with the Lord, take an hour-long walk in the morning or evening, leave the office early and go to the local park).

3. Acts 3:19–20 speaks of Christ's second coming as a "season of refreshment." Based upon our study, in what ways will Christ's return bring about rest?

4. Is there an area in your life that is creating anxiety (e.g., ministry opportunity, an assignment at work or school)? Claim the truth of 1 Peter 5:7.

4

Jeremiah
All Alone in a Couple's World

When Jeremiah said, in his people's hour of direst need, that "houses and fields and [vineyards] shall again be bought in this land," it was a token of confidence in the future. That requires faith, and may God grant us it daily. I don't mean the faith that flees the world, but the faith that endures in the world and loves and remains true to the world in spite of all the hardships it brings us.

—Dietrich Bonhoeffer, 1906–1945
(a single German theologian and pastor executed for his
opposition to the Nazi government)

"'How long, Lord, will you continue to ignore me? How long will you pay no attention to me?' Oh, Lord, these words of Psalm 13 haunt the very core of my being. I know theologically you are with me, but the cries of my heart far outweigh the cognitive. Lord, I feel so isolated and alone."

These words were lifted from the journal written during my first year of doctoral studies in Scotland. After saying farewell to my family and friends, I arrived at a location where I knew no one. I gave up a job that I loved and the comforts of the United States to live in a dormitory inhabited primarily by undergraduates. The pangs of emptiness and isolation failed to dissipate despite the busyness of my studies. The glamour of living abroad and studying at a university founded only four years after Christopher Columbus discovered the Americas quickly disappeared. Instead, I was left with an enormous void—I felt empty and longed for intimacy.

My loneliness was further exacerbated by the fact that nearly all of the doctoral students were married; the support and intimacy that stem from marriage were absent in my life. Rather than being met by the loving embrace of a spouse, I returned home to a flat, often accompanied by immature Greek teenagers. Now please understand I have nothing against Greeks or teenagers, but a culture that enjoys dinner at 10 P.M. and encourages bedtime at 2 or 3 A.M. is far from appropriate for graduate studies. As time progressed, my loneliness evolved into bitterness and jealousy.

Compared to my time in Aberdeen, my loneliness is far milder and less frequent now, yet I still find myself relying on the "Prozac of loneliness"—busyness. Working long hours drowns out my soul's longings and distracts me from my inadequacies. Instead of defining my existence by marriage and children, I utilize events and accomplishments. This "stiff-arm" toward relationships and an air of independence buffer any appearances of vulnerability.

Reticence surrounds my disclosure for I have grown in my acceptance of being alone. In fact, I now value my singleness and the times when I can steal away to think, meditate, and unwind after a day spent surrounded by and giving to people. But it would be misleading to deny that loneliness has been an issue in my life and that on occasion the cloud of isolation will revisit. I also feel it is important to share because I know that many singles share this plight. A recent e-mail I received reinforces this belief. The single adult confesses, "I grapple with my singleness because I don't like being alone. I long to have a close relationship with someone. I want to know that someone trusts me and takes an interest in me." Such feelings are echoed time and time again by single adults.

Loneliness has been defined as "a chronic distressful mental state whereby an individual feels estranged from or rejected by peers and is starved for the emotional intimacy found in relationships and mutual activity."[1] Frequently this subjective experience stems from a change in a living situation, the loss of a spouse through death or divorce, or the onset of a disability.[2] For many singles, the prospect of growing old with no one to provide for them fuels this mental state; most married individuals have children and grandchildren who can and will care for them, not to mention the joy that comes from rocking children to sleep or being entertained by grandchildren. Another possible underlying reason for loneliness is that the absence of a partner provides no outlet for emotional and physical intimacy. Whatever the case, loneliness can result in isolation, fear, depression, lack of self-worth, emptiness, and even anger and bitterness. In recent years, researchers have demonstrated that loneliness can even alter cardiac function, disrupt sleeping patterns, cause higher blood pressure, and diminish ability to fight diseases.[3]

Jeremiah: A Perfect Model

Few biblical characters had more reason to be lonely than the prophet Jeremiah. He belonged to a priestly family which had long been ousted from the religious and royal establishment.[4] In addition to his embarrassing lineage, Jeremiah was called at birth to serve as a prophet during the most devastating events in Jewish history. Prophesying from the thirteenth year of Josiah's reign (627 B.C.) until shortly after the fall of Jerusalem in 587 B.C., his forty-year ministry was marked by opponents' attempts to silence him by means of arrests, trials, beatings, imprisonments, and even assassination plots (e.g., Jer. 26:10–19; 36:26; 37:11–38:6). Throughout the book, the prophet lamented to God and even called down judgment on the opposition (e.g., 11:19–20; 20:10–12) and earned his title, the "weeping prophet" (see 9:1; 13:17; 14:17).

While public ridicule of his message was swift and extreme, the prophet's personal sacrifices were far greater than any public outcry. His life's experiences were crafted to reflect God's revelation to the people of Judah. For instance, his prophetic office included the command to remain single. The Lord instructed Jeremiah, "You shall not take a wife, nor shall you have sons or daughters in this place" (Jer. 16:2 NRSV). As pointed out by one biblical scholar, "Hosea's marriage is shocking (Hos. 1:2), but not unheard of. Jeremiah's bachelorhood, however, is so unusual among the Jews that the Old Testament has no word for bachelor, and it undoubtedly reinforces questions about him."[5] Terence Fretheim, in his recent commentary on the book of

Jeremiah, adds, "Given the importance of children in that culture, this prohibition would have been startling to both prophet and people."[6] To further complicate matters, Jeremiah was also to refrain from attending social events, such as funerals and weddings (Jer. 16:5–9). His life was consumed with fulfilling his prophetic role. One Old Testament scholar notes,

> Jeremiah serves God not only with the harsh proclamation of his mouth, but also with his person; his life becomes unexpectedly involved in the cause of God on earth. Thus, now—and in Jeremiah this is something new—the prophet not only becomes a witness of God through the strength of his charisma, but also in his humanity; but not as one who triumphs over the sins of mankind, not as one overcoming, but as a messenger of God to mankind breaking under the strain. Hence, Jeremiah's life here becomes a forceful witness, his suffering soul and his life ebbing away in God's service becomes a testimony of God.[7]

Jeremiah endured the absence of a spouse or family, removal from all social events, and a thankless and despised profession—few individuals in this world have had greater reasons to embrace loneliness. How did this "prophet of loneliness" continue to live life, let alone continue to be obedient to the Lord? Thankfully, the book of Jeremiah provides a wonderful glimpse into the life of this Old Testament saint. While this prophet did struggle with life, anxious thoughts, and fears, Jeremiah displays five ways to persevere and continue despite living alone.

Means to Address Loneliness

Recognition of God's Calling

In *The Fellowship of the Ring*, Frodo protests to Gandalf crying, "I am not made for perilous quests. I wish I had never seen the Ring! Why did it come to me? Why was I chosen?" Gandalf replies, "Such questions cannot be answered. You may be sure that it was not for any merit that others do not possess; not for power or wisdom, at any rate. But you have been chosen and you must therefore use such strength and heart and wits as you have."[8]

Like Frodo, Jeremiah was called. In fact, the opening words of the book inform us that Jeremiah was appointed before birth for this assignment. The Lord states in 1:5 (NRSV), "Before I formed you in the womb I knew you, and before you were born I consecrated you; I appointed you a prophet to the nations." Reminiscent of Moses, Jeremiah questions his own ability to live up to God's appointed position. However, the Lord quickly assures Jeremiah that he is the man for the task. In the midst of lonely times and trying periods of ministry, Jeremiah could return to these words for comfort and encouragement. Jeremiah's prophetic office was not bequeathed out of charity or by default, but because God ordained it. When it might have appeared that no one cared about him, Jeremiah could reflect on the fact that the God of the universe knew him. This knowledge and calling bore no strings, no preconditions, and no contract.

As believers, we also have the great assurance of knowing that God called us prior to birth. Ephesians 1:4–6 (NRSV) reads, "Just as [God] chose us in Christ before the foundation of the world to be holy and blameless before him in love. He destined us for adoption as his children through Jesus Christ, according to the good pleasure of his will, to the praise of his glorious grace that he freely bestowed on us in the Beloved." The Lord sought us and appointed us to be His ambassadors. During times of loneliness, I quickly forget the wonderful truth that the Creator of the universe, the Almighty God, knows and cares for me. It is the Father who loved me when I was unwilling and unable to respond. His Son became flesh so that I might become His child. In his well-written and challenging book on the prophet Jeremiah, Eugene Peterson writes,

> Before Jeremiah knew God, God knew Jeremiah: "Before I formed you in the womb I knew you." This turns everything we ever thought about God around. We think that God is an object about which we have questions. We are curious about God. We make inquiries about God. We read books about God. We

> get into late night bull sessions about God. We drop
> into church from time to time to see what is going
> on with God. We indulge in an occasional sunset or
> symphony to cultivate a feeling of reverence for God.
> But that is not the reality of our lives with God.[9]

Note that God also grants provisions in accordance with the calling. The Lord promised Jeremiah that he would be delivered from his enemies (1:8) and that he would receive the necessary words to speak (1:9). And while at times Jeremiah doubted, the Lord supplied.

Occasionally the gift of singleness seems too much to bear. Waiting for the Lord and remaining content with life despite my present state seems overwhelming. I long to know someone intimately and for someone to know me. May we not forget that we have a God who does know us intimately and longs for our affection. C. S. Lewis aptly states,

> God is both further from us, and nearer to us, than
> any other being. He is further from us because of the
> sheer difference between that which has Its principle
> of being in Itself and that to which being is communi-
> cated in one compared with which the difference be-
> tween an archangel and a worm is quite significant.
> He makes, we are made: He is original, we deriva-
> tive. But at the same time, and for the same reason,
> the intimacy between God and even the meanest
> creature is closer than any that creatures can attain
> with one another.[10]

As noted by David in Psalm 68, the Lord cares for us and "makes a home for the lonely" (v. 6 NASB). And in the New Testament we are reminded that this same loving God will never leave us, nor abandon us (see Heb. 13:5).

Trust in God's Control

To know the truth is one thing, but to act upon it is quite another. Despite the certainty of God's love and His calling, the words of

Samuel Taylor Coleridge's "The Rime of the Ancient Mariner" seem more accurate:

> *Alone, alone, all, all alone,*
> *Alone on a wide wide sea!*
> *And never a saint took pity on*
> *My soul in agony. . . .*

> *This soul hath been*
> *alone on a wide wide sea;*
> *So lonely 'twas, that God himself*
> *Scarce seemed there to be.*

'Tis a wonderful thing to know that Jesus loves me, but the events of life and the lack of companionship often suggest otherwise. Questions remain unanswered in this sea of loneliness: If Jesus truly loved me, could He not at least provide one or two close friends as I bear this "gift" of singleness? If Jesus truly loved me, couldn't He remove some of the pain that stems from the loss of my spouse? If Jesus truly loved me, couldn't He eliminate some of the financial burdens in raising my two children all alone? And the list could continue . . .

Jeremiah raised similar questions during his time of ministry. Recognizing that the Lord knows him (15:15), the weeping prophet proceeds to remind the Lord of his various services rendered—suffering for the Lord's sake, acceptance of and rejoicing in the Lord's words, remaining alone in his stance for the Lord, and enduring hardships for His cause (15:15–17). In just three verses, the prophet refers to himself approximately fifteen times and states that each action was specifically performed on behalf of the Lord. He concludes his rehearsal of all that he has accomplished for God by questioning the very character of God. He cries out, "Why is my pain unceasing, my wound incurable, refusing to be healed? Truly, you are to me like a deceitful brook, like waters that fail" (15:18 NRSV). The reference to a "deceitful brook" recalls the idea of a sojourner in a desert who observes the appearance of a brook in the distance—only to discover upon arrival that it was a mirage. In effect, Jeremiah demands from the Lord an explanation. Is God really true to His word? Is God reliable? Where is God when one of His prophets needs relief? One scholar writes,

Though Jeremiah's complaint may be physical or psychological in orientation (see chs. 36–38), this language seems to refer to the effects of his troubles on his entire person. That his antagonists persecute him and even seek to kill him, and relationships with his own friends and family are severely ruptured, causes a deep, ongoing pain; no resolution to his persecution and isolation seems possible.[11]

The Lord's response to Jeremiah in the subsequent verses reminds me of a mother interacting with her toddler. The Lord lovingly and patiently reassures and reaffirms the basic promises He made to Jeremiah in chapter 1. If Jeremiah returns to his prophetic calling and to the uttering of God's words, he will be delivered from his enemies. The Lord will not allow Jeremiah's oppressors to take his life.

Trusting in God despite the circumstances requires meditation upon His promises and reflection upon His past actions. Earlier we observed Psalm 13 where David, like Jeremiah, questions God's love and ability to provide.[12] As David progresses with this lament, he recognizes that God's Word is sure and that the Lord has dealt graciously and generously in the past. Our trust is not rooted in false hope or fanciful dreams. Our confidence in the Lord's love for us and His all-powerful hand resides in who He is and what He has done in our lives. Despite bouts of loneliness and the knowledge that he would always be single (16:1–9), Jeremiah confidently declares that the Lord is "my strength, and my fortress, and my refuge in the day of affliction" (16:19 KJV). He continues this praise of God, pronouncing that one who trusts in the Lord and places hope in Him will be blessed (17:7).

Possession of God's Perspective

Possessing God's perspective is key to trusting in the Lord. While Jeremiah wrestled with life and his role as a prophet, he remained faithful to the Lord—not because the Lord eased his pain or brought a "significant other" into his life, but because Jeremiah ultimately recognized that his suffering and the judgment upon the people of Judah were temporary. One biblical scholar notes, "The prophet does not see the world from the point of view of a political theory; he is a person who sees the world from the point of view of God; he sees the world through the eyes of God."[13]

This acknowledgment of the Lord and His ways is vividly portrayed in Jeremiah's purchase of a field during the Babylonians' besiegement of Jerusalem just before its fall in 586 B.C. This expenditure in the midst of such political and economic crises probably solidified the criticisms and opinions of Jeremiah's antagonists. What initially seemed a foolish investment demonstrated Jeremiah's trust in the Lord's promise that one day his descendents would return to the land. This scene concludes with a prayer (32:16–25) where the prophet asserts,

> Ah Lord GOD! It is you who made the heavens and the earth by your great power and by your outstretched arm! Nothing is too hard for you. You show steadfast love to the thousandth generation, but repay the guilt of parents into the laps of their children after them, O great and mighty God whose name is the LORD of hosts, great in counsel and mighty in deed; whose eyes are open to all the ways of mortals, rewarding all according to their ways and according to the fruit of their doings. (vv. 17–19 NRSV)

Because Jeremiah understood the wondrous deeds God had performed in the past, he could be certain that nothing in the future was insurmountable for the Lord. This prophet looked to the eternal rather than the temporal.

A key problem of loneliness resides in the fact that we have lost sight of God's plan and purpose for our lives. Warren Wiersbe in his book *Lonely People* defines loneliness as "the malnutrition of the soul that results from living on substitutes."[14] In some of my darkest hours of living solo, I have experienced my most intimate times with the Lord. During those difficult days of my first year in Aberdeen, the Lord revealed Himself in numerous ways. One event I will never forget happened near the end of an extremely trying week. My research had grown stagnate and was as enjoyable as a root canal. The weather had been true to Aberdeen tradition—cold and wet. The crime rate in Scotland was about to rise as I contemplated murdering my Greek flat mates. And my bank account had dwindled so low that the account cost more than it contained. In fact, my financial state was so desperate that I had decided to save some pennies by forgoing lunches that week. Around lunchtime on Thursday I had almost reached my limit. I was walking down main street praying for strength and contentment when down at my feet, I saw a ten pound note. As I picked it up, I found another ten pound bill. It was obvious from their condition that the bills had lain there for some time. I could not believe my eyes! While I stood there stunned, a lady passed by and noticed what I had discovered. Unable to control myself, I said, "Isn't the Lord good?!" The lady looked at me as if I had just been released from a mental ward. That afternoon, I had a wonderful hot meal in the student cafeteria—a great reminder of the awesome God we serve.

The difficult periods of life serve as the anvil God utilizes to fashion and mold us into His image. Paul writes in Romans 5:3–5 (NRSV), "And not only that, but we also boast in our sufferings, knowing that suffering produces endurance, and endurance produces character, and character produces hope, and hope does not disappoint us, because God's love has been poured into our hearts through the Holy Spirit that has been given to us." Living alone in this world is often painful. Few people understood this better than the prophet Jeremiah. And yet, Jeremiah had the marvelous opportunity to serve as the Lord's spokesperson, to witness firsthand the Lord's provision, and to walk in intimacy with God. The great theologian of the twentieth century, Karl Barth, notes,

> If we fix our eyes upon the place where the course of the world reaches its lowest point, where its vanity is unmistakable, where its groanings are most bitter and the divine incognito most impenetrable, we shall encounter there—Jesus Christ. . . . The transformation of all things occurs where the riddle of human life reaches its culminating point. The hope of His glory emerges for us when nothing but the existentiality of God remains, and He becomes to us the veritable

and living God. He whom we can apprehend only as against us, stands there—for us.[15]

A Value of Prayer

Ongoing communion with the Lord is essential to maintaining God's perspective. We observed in a previous section that prayer provides the venue for reflection upon who the Lord is and His past and present actions. The prophet recounts God's faithful and powerful hand in the lives of the Jewish people. Jeremiah reflects on a holy and loving God who demands obedience. Prayer also serves as a vehicle for wisdom and clarification from God as we take time to listen. Jeremiah's prayer concludes chapter 32 with "Yet you, O Lord GOD, have said to me, 'Buy the field for money and get witnesses'—though the city has been given into the hands of the Chaldeans" (32:25 NRSV). In his attempt to unravel his confusion over the Lord's command, Jeremiah speaks honestly with the Lord, asking for understanding.

The prophet's prayer life demonstrates his intimacy with God. Jeremiah could speak freely to the Lord concerning issues. As seen above, he felt free to question the Lord. And, elsewhere, Jeremiah even expresses anger as he prays to the Lord (e.g., 12:1–2; 20:7). In this, the most autobiographical prophetic book, we find the author communicating with the Lord on a profound level. Eugene Peterson writes,

> No one becomes human the way Jeremiah was human by posing in a posture of victory. It was his prayers, hidden but persistent, that brought him to the human wholeness and spiritual sensitivity that we want. What we do in secret determines the soundness of who we are in public. Prayer is the secret work that develops a life that is thoroughly authentic and deeply human.[16]

Jeremiah's prayer life also testifies to the Lord's desire for communication with us. The Lord declares to the people of Judah, "'When you call out to me and come to me in prayer, I will hear your prayers. When you seek me in prayer and worship, you will find me available to you. If you seek me with all your heart and soul, I will make myself available to you,' says the LORD" (29:12–14a). God's intention prior to the Fall was for man and woman to fellowship with Him. God's longing was so great that He provided a means for this fellowship to be restored—a means that cost Him His very own Son. Through Scripture, "prophet and psalmist alike teach us very firmly that the right way to deal with doubt and protest within the soul is to carry them straight to God and never let them carry us away from him. God is his own interpreter, and he will make things plain."[17] When loneliness assails us, we must admit our feelings to the Lord. He will draw near to the one who runs to Him (James 4:8).

An Appreciation of Friends

As demonstrated in our look at the apostle Paul, both unmarried and married companions are essential parts of living life for the Lord. Similarly, Jeremiah benefited from the presence of several individuals in his life. One of these who is significant for our study is an Ethiopian slave named Ebed Melech (38:1–13). A eunuch in the king's court, Ebed Melech hears that Jeremiah has been thrown into a waterless, but muddy, cistern. Without food or water, the prophet was abandoned, left to die for encouraging the Jews to surrender to the Babylonians—action tantamount to treason. Alone, floods of emotions undoubtedly plagued Jeremiah. *How will anyone be able to find me in this obscure location? Will anyone care enough to come to my rescue?*

I doubt Jeremiah would have ever dreamed that an Ethiopian slave would be the one to rescue him. Ebed Melech risked his own life as he confronted King Zedekiah and requested that the king remove Jeremiah from the pit. Ebed Melech then personally oversaw the rescue of the prophet, ensuring that Jeremiah was unharmed in the process (e.g., the use of rags and scraps of clothing to ease Jeremiah's extrication). How ironic that only a foreigner, single I might add, cared enough to rescue the abandoned prophet!

Other individuals who support Jeremiah throughout the book include Gedaliah, the governor of Judah, who ensured political safety for Jeremiah (40:5–6); Elasah, the son of Shaphan, who risked his own life to deliver a letter for Jeremiah (29:1–3); Baruch, who served Jeremiah, forfeiting his royal lineage, prosperity, security, and peace (32:13–15; 36:4–26); and the prophet Uriah of Kiriath Jearim, who was executed for aligning himself with Jeremiah (26:20–23).

I have found that during my times of loneliness, I so easily overlook the people the Lord has strategically and graciously placed in my life. While most of my doctoral work was completed at the University of Aberdeen, one year of my studies was spent at the Universitätsstadt in Tübingen, Germany. It was here that the Lord provided me with one of life's "Ebed Melechs." I am fairly confident that even to this day, Sigurd Kaiser has no idea how much the friendship of him and his wife meant to me during my year of studies in Tübingen. My first weeks in Germany contained many embarrassing and trying moments. Struggling to speak German, I needed to register at the university, open a bank account, purchase groceries, and learn the social taboos of living in the Albrecht-Bengel Haus, a residency primarily for theological students. Sigurd not only interrupted his busy schedule to assist me, but also showed Christ's love as he cared for so many of my needs. His companionship pushed the shadows of loneliness into the far recesses of my soul.

Granted, the presence of people does not necessarily remove the possibility of loneliness. In fact, statistics show that many married people are lonely. But we were designed and saved for the purpose of community. We need one another as members of the family of God. Unfortunately, our society encourages and applauds Lone Rangers. In a most revealing book, Laura Pappano shares these profound insights into our culture:

> The picture is a rather dismal one. Instead of using energy and money to make a difference for everyone, people tend to be isolationist, improving life within their personal territory . . . feelings of discontent and disconnection do not draw people to seek solace in each other but to venture out to find a salve in the marketplace. There, of course, it is sold as a pint of gourmet ice cream or a new shade of lipstick. It is beautifully packaged and ready to take home. But it doesn't last long.[18]

In Pappano's final assessment, she proposes we must find

opportunities to reach out. I believe she is correct. To have friends one must show himself or herself to be friendly (Prov. 18:24 KJV). And yet, you might echo the response of a single adult who retorted,

> I was born again as a result of being divorced so I praise the Lord for my divorce. I try to be a blessing, but I am so lonely. Sometimes you get tired of giving, of hurting and you just want to talk and fit in. As for fitting in, forget it. No one understands, because they are couple-oriented. How could they?[19]

I recognize that not everyone will understand. Certainly Jeremiah faced so-called friends who not only misunderstood him but even sought to kill him (e.g., 20:2, 10–11; 34:17; 38:1–4). Nevertheless, I would argue that one of the provisions the Lord can and will make for us is people. If nothing else, you have been placed into His family and you are now part of a Christian community. There were periods when Jeremiah was alone and when he struggled with loneliness; but the prophet also experienced companionship and devotion.

Conclusion

The life of Jeremiah continues to amaze me. In spite of all that he experienced, Jeremiah never quit. His resolve to be obedient to his calling is both convicting and challenging. Jeremiah's single pursuit in life was to listen to what God said about knowing His grace (9:24; cf. Phil. 3:10; John 17:3). Frequently alone and at times lonely, the weeping prophet continued to minister to the Jewish people.

We have observed five areas that allowed this single adult to serve productively in a married world. First, Jeremiah recognized that the Lord had called him. The God of the universe was specifically interested in and loved Jeremiah. As we noted, the New Testament also indicates that we as believers have been chosen before the foundation of the world. The Lord's love for us should serve as a great source of encouragement. Second, Jeremiah's trust in God's control served as a defense against loneliness. He only needed to reflect on the Lord's past record to know of His faithfulness and power. Paul writes in Romans 8 that the God who called us before the foundation of the world will see that we are ultimately glorified. Third, Jeremiah was able to press on because he possessed God's perspective. Jeremiah recognized the Lord's plan and purpose for his life. Difficult periods of life can yield great benefits. Jeremiah's commitment to prayer serves as the fourth way in which the prophet was able to handle loneliness. Constant communion with the Lord assists in tuning our will to His. It also allows for an avenue to express to the Lord our concerns and frustrations. Finally, Jeremiah benefited from the presence of people in his life. He depended on Ebed Melech and others, such as Baruch, who served with him for over twenty years. As demonstrated even in our look at the apostle Paul, both unmarried and married companions are an essential component to living life for the Lord.

For Reflection

1. Spend some time reading and reflecting on Psalm 13. What kinds of experiences cause you to think that God has forgotten you? Then ask yourself, What are some examples of how God has been faithful in my life?
2. How effective is my prayer life for fixing my eyes on the Lord?
3. The psalmist writes, "Whom have I in heaven but You? And besides You, I desire nothing on earth. My flesh and my heart may fail, but God is the strength of my heart and my portion forever" (Ps. 73:25–26 NASB). How does it affect your daily life to know that the Lord is the rock of your heart?
4. Make a list of individuals whom the Lord has used in your life (e.g., a particular friend, a family member, a pastor, a teacher, a coworker). Thank the Lord for these precious gifts. You may want to write notes to these people expressing how much they mean to you.

5

Ruth

Encountering Shattered Dreams

> Nothing less will shake a man—or at any rate a man
> like me—out of his merely verbal thinking and his
> merely notional beliefs. He has to be knocked silly
> before he comes to his senses. Only torture will bring
> out the truth. Only under torture does he discover it
> himself.
>
> —C. S. Lewis, 1898–1963
> (a confirmed bachelor who married only four years before
> the death of his wife, Joy Davidman)

The Christian world was stunned. A group of armed Islamic sepa-
ratists, Abu Sayyaf, had kidnapped New Tribes missionaries Martin and Gracia Burnham. For eighteen months family and friends
waited. Then the horrible happened. In the attempt to rescue the
hostages, forty-two-year-old Martin was killed and forty-three-
year-old Gracia was wounded in the leg. Instead of joy and glad-
ness, the liberated prisoner had only shock and anguish. For the
hostage ordeal to end with the death of her husband seemed unjust.

Perhaps you have not lost your spouse, but you understand vanished hopes, shattered dreams, or cruel injustice. Whether through a
divorce or the termination of a serious dating relationship, you have
experienced the painful and paralyzing blow of a shattered dream.
As you attempt to pick up the pieces in the aftermath, questions swirl

through your mind. How could this have happened? What could I have done differently? Where do I go from here?

Left as a widow with no children, Ruth undoubtedly was asking similar questions. Ruth, a Moabite woman, was married for ten years, but now alone, her pain was almost insurmountable; her hopes and dreams for a lifetime were razed in a brief period of time. Let us examine her life and the means that allowed her to address these heartbreaks of life.

Shredded Dreams and Unfulfilled Expectations

The historical setting of the book of Ruth is the time of the judges— an era marked by a cycle of sin, slavery, and salvation. Everyone did "what was right in their own eyes." Nestled in this age of violent invasions, apostate religion, unchecked lawlessness, and civil war rests the small, but powerful story of Ruth. This romantic story provides a moral contrast to the period as it reveals the strength of its characters and provides a plot with a peaceful resolution. In so doing, the book demonstrates God's guidance in the lives of His people and His provision of a future king through Ruth and Boaz.

The introduction (1:1–6) functions as the backdrop to this book. The tragic deaths of Ruth's father-in-law, her brother-in-law, and, most significantly, her husband startle the reader. Ruth's tapestry of life was unraveling before her eyes. Her husband, her lifetime partner, had died. For ten years they had experienced life together. The reader is also surprised to learn that during this ten-year period of marriage, Ruth and Mahlon had no children. It was after ten years of barrenness that Sarai gave her Egyptian maid, Hagar, to Abram (Gen. 16:3). As pointed out by Robert Hubbard Jr. in his commentary on the book of Ruth, "If the audience understood ten years as the customary period given a couple to produce children before taking alternative, remedial steps, then the reference to ten years here slightly heightens the narrative's tension."[1]

The predicament in which Ruth finds herself presents extreme difficulty and even danger in the Near Eastern world. She lacks the provision and protection of a husband in a patriarchal society. In addition, she also has no children, the source of security and care for a widow. The numerous regulations providing for widows and orphans in the Old Testament testify to this fact. Exodus 22:22–24 warns, "You must not afflict any widow or orphan. If you afflict them in any way, and they cry to me, I will surely hear their cry. And my anger will burn and I will kill you with the sword, and your wives will be widows and your children will be fatherless." Ruth not only lost her companion and lover; she is now responsible for the practical concerns of daily living—and for her future. The threads of the tapestry lay strewn across the room.

Strengthened Determination and Unfailing Devotion

Repairing an unraveled tapestry involves skill and patience. It takes an expert to replace worn threads with new ones. The condition of Ruth's life by verse 17 is one of frayed threads—hopes, expectations, and life's dreams are in tatters. How could this young Moabite widow continue?

What proves more remarkable than the tragedies in her life is the manner in which Ruth responds. Marked by three distinct threads, the tapestry of Ruth's life becomes a beautiful testimony to the gracious hand of the Divine Weaver. Let us observe how, instead of being discarded, Ruth faces her circumstances with a sacrifice to personal preferences, a faithful adherence to commitment, and an embracement of hope rooted in her deep faith.

Marked by an Expression of Sacrificial Love

With no more ties in Moab and the end of the famine in Israel, Naomi was left with few options but to return to her homeland. Twice she pleads with her daughters-in-law to remain in Moab, and in a heart-wrenching scene Orpah finally agrees to return to her home while Ruth swears allegiance to her mother-in-law. Orpah's departure prompts a second round of great weeping (1:14; also, cf. 1:9). This loud lamenting typifies times of mourning in the Old Testament (e.g., Judg. 21:2; 2 Sam. 13:36; Job 2:12) and speaks of the pain and difficulty in the parting of the women after all of these years.

One would expect that Ruth would follow Orpah. Instead, she proclaims to Naomi:

> For wherever you go, I will go. Wherever you live,
> I will live. Your people will become my people, and
> your God will become my God. Wherever you die,
> I will die—and there I will be buried. May the Lord
> punish me severely if I do not keep my promise! Only
> death will be able to separate me from you! (1:16–17)

These words declared by Ruth to her mother-in-law are nothing short of amazing. Ruth understood the gravity of her oath to remain with Naomi. She was forgoing the opportunity for another spouse, the comfort and safety of her homeland, and the security and love of a family. Naomi also recognized this sacrifice of the security of a home with a new husband and the importance of Ruth's people and religion when, for the third time, Naomi commanded Ruth to leave her and return to Moab. Naomi lacked the provision and protection of a husband and the opportunity to provide a new husband for Ruth. This is why she told her daughters-in-law, "Each of you should return to your mother's home!" (1:8). The reference to "mother's house," rather than the typical phrase "father's house" suggests her mother's bedroom—the place where marriages were arranged.[2] After Rebekah conversed with Abraham's servant concerning a wife for Isaac, she ran to her "mother's household" to report the proposal (Gen. 24:28). Naomi pleads with Ruth to return to Moab where she would more than likely find another spouse and have a family.

Astonishment at Ruth's decision also stems from the difficulties of traveling to the land of Israel as a foreigner. She must have feared loneliness, being ostracized, and even threats to her personal safety since a Moabite was a second-class citizen in Israel. While Jews were not forbidden to marry these descendants of Lot (cf. Deut. 7:1–3),[3] the Lord did forbid Moabites from entering the congregation of the Lord (Deut. 23:3). Certainly Ruth's marital status and lack of children also complicated matters. Boaz's directions to his servants to leave Ruth alone (Ruth 2:9) only confirm her precarious position.

Another shocking factor surrounding Ruth's decision stems from her willingness to "cling"[4] to her mother-in-law and sacrifice on her behalf. Naomi was swimming in a vat of her own self-pity and bitterness and was quite possibly not an easy character to love at this point in her life. She accuses the Lord of attacking her (1:13), treating her harshly (v. 20), leaving her empty-handed, opposing her, and making her suffer (v. 21). In short, Naomi credits the Lord as the source of all her tragedies. If anything, you would have thought Ruth would have avoided following Naomi in case this God inflicts further tragedies. Naomi's questionable faith in Yahweh may also be observed in her making no attempt to return to Israel during ten years in Moab, returning to Israel for mere pragmatic reasons, and encouraging her daughters-in-law to worship the Moabite god, Chemosh. Old Testament scholar Katharine Doob Sakenfeld notes two important connections with the stories of the patriarchs and the book of Job in Naomi's cry in verses 20–21. She observes,

> With respect to Genesis, it elucidates the content of her cry as a reversal of blessing in the face of bereavement—the loss of offspring and her self-renaming, as well as the story's larger motif of kingship. With respect to Job, it suggests that her bitterness is fueled not just by the fact of her loss, but also by her own sense of integrity and innocence in the face of God's inexplicable action. She has lost not only her husband and sons, but also her way of making sense of her life.[5]

One would have thought that the words of this so-called believing Israelite, a daughter of Abraham, would have stopped Ruth from taking one step further toward the land of Judah.

Naomi's bitterness also affects her attitude toward Ruth. Upon returning to Bethlehem, Naomi asks to be called *Mara*, meaning "bitter," because "I left here full, but the Lord has caused me to return empty-handed" (1:21). Every time I read Naomi's words I pause in amazement and disgust. Even in her emotional distress, how could she forget her daughter-in-law standing beside her? Naomi's calloused remarks also fail to recognize that her dead son was also Ruth's husband. I can only imagine what Ruth was thinking as these unappreciative words rolled off the lips of her mother-in-law. One also wonders why, when these women settled in Bethlehem, it was Ruth, not Ruth and Naomi, who was in the fields gleaning barley. Naomi's health could not have been that poor—she had made the long journey across the Jordan Rift Valley from Moab. While the narrative does mention Naomi's assistance in obtaining Boaz (3:1–6), it never mentions Naomi's gratitude to her daughter-in-law or her recognition of Ruth's commitment to her.

The older I become and the longer I am single, the more I find Ruth's personal sacrifices convicting and, might I confess, a bit masochistic. Naomi's self-pity would have grown old very quickly, and her ingratitude would have been sufficient for me to pack my bags and join Orpah on the road back to Moab. And yet, Ruth's sacrificial love for Naomi displays a woman of great beauty. Boaz, on the eve that he finds Ruth at his side, blesses her, stating, "May you be rewarded by the LORD, dear woman! This act of devotion is greater than what you did before. For you have not sought to marry one of the young men, whether poor or rich. . . . Everyone in the village knows that you are a worthy woman" (3:10–11). We will discuss in the next section her level of commitment, but we would be remiss not to note Boaz's description of Ruth. He could not use a better word to embody Ruth's sacrificial giving of herself than the word *hesed*, "devotion." This Hebrew word indicates loyalty, faithfulness, and goodness. Normally the term refers to the Lord's action toward His people (see 1:8; 2:20). Hubbard defines the term as "rare, risky, and restrictive, the practice of loyal, compassionate devotion."[6] Only this type of love could be willing to forego one's personal preferences and life's expected norms for another person.

Recently, a married friend was speaking of men who never marry and how they are usually eccentric—adults caught up in their own little world. I had to smile when, in the midst of his pontificating, he realized what he was saying and quickly exempted me from the "norm." What a relief to know that I had been relegated to the realm of the married, or should I say, the "normal." While I recognize that singleness can serve as a breeding ground for self-centeredness, the issue lies at the root of much of humanity's sin—married or single. The greatest in the kingdom of God are not equated with those who act from passion nor from greed, but with those who take the position of humility and self-sacrifice (e.g., Matt. 23:11; Luke 22:24–27). Upon washing the feet of the disciples, Jesus instructs His band of men, "For I have given you an example—you should do just as I have done for you. I tell you the solemn truth, the slave is not greater than his master, nor is the one who is sent as a messenger greater than the one who sent him. If you understand these things, you will be blessed if you do them" (John 13:15–17). Our Redeemer and Master set the model. It was He who humbled Himself even to the point of death—the death of a cross (Phil. 2:6–11). In the midst of shredded dreams, it can be a struggle to look outward. Our eyes turn upon ourselves, inspecting the wounds. Ruth could have been like her mother-in-law and drowned in her own pain and loss. It is easy to be a Naomi—but our calling is far nobler.

Marked by a Faithful Adherence to a Commitment

I had the "brilliant" idea of building a garden shed from a picture unearthed in a gardening magazine. Recognizing my lack of construction skills and experience, I decided it would be wise to enlist some assistance. My father graciously agreed to draw the blueprints, and, as is usual for my father, he went well beyond the call of duty, providing such superb details that I fondly labeled the blueprints "The Idiot's Guide to Building a Garden Tool Shed." I also recruited a student, providing him with free lodging and pesos in exchange for his expertise and youthful energy. The team was complete. The only catch was that the student was only available to assist for two weeks. While this should have been ample time to complete this structural masterpiece, because of the weather, my lack of experience, inadequate equipment (i.e., no truck), and the student's prior commitments, the tool shed failed to make completion date. When the student left, the task was mine to finish. Days passed and my resolve to complete the building began to wane. Commitment was easy when we were talking two weeks, but by week four, I was sick of staring at the incomplete creation.

Ben Patterson writes in his thought-provoking book, *Waiting: Finding Hope When God Seems Silent*, "One huge, heroic act would be easier than a lifetime of little daily decisions, especially when it may take a lifetime to discover that the promises of God were worth the no we said to ourselves and to the world each day."[7] True commitment demonstrates itself on the anvils of time and trouble. Committing to building a garden tool shed might sound grand, but its true greatness is only revealed when the commitment is lived out—over an extended period of time and through the adverse circumstances that surrounded the building of this *Better Homes and Gardens* master-piece. Ruth's willingness to follow Naomi is commendable, but her faithfulness to that commitment despite the circumstances speaks of courage and character.

Before examining her fortitude in carrying out her commitment, we need to observe the commitment itself. In Ruth's declaration to follow Naomi, she commits to going wherever Naomi may go, residing wherever Naomi resides, abandoning the Moabite people for the Israelite nation, and forsaking Chemosh for Yahweh. To ensure her dedication, Ruth states that she will not only be there until Naomi dies, but until Ruth herself passes away. In other words, Ruth will be buried with Naomi and her people. In her commentary on the book of Ruth, Katharine Doob Sakenfeld makes an excellent point:

> In cultures of the ancient Near East, burial in one's ancestral homeland was considered extremely im-portant. The biblical narrative of the transporting of Joseph's bones back from Egypt to land purchased by his father Jacob (Joshua 24:32; cf. Gen. 50:24–26) illustrates this tradition. By insisting that she will be buried with Naomi, Ruth is further distancing her-self from her homeland.[8]

Ruth further guarantees the fulfillment of her words by calling on the Lord to punish her if she does not carry through with her promise to Naomi. Ruth's proclamation of devotion severs her life in Moab and launches her into an unsure future. "Now she is to leave her people and join the Israelite people juridically and religiously in a new context that comprises the most important elements in life: land, grave, people, and faith."[9]

Time validated Ruth's oath of allegiance to Naomi. First, Ruth maintained her commitment in the midst of Naomi's ingratitude. We have already noted the women's arrival in Bethlehem and Naomi's lack of acknowledgment of her daughter-in-law's presence. The nar-rator seems to suggest this as he once again reiterates, "So Naomi returned, accompanied by her Moabite daughter-in-law Ruth, who came back with her from the region of Moab" (1:22).

A second demonstration of Ruth's faithful adherence to her

words of promise is displayed in her hard work. The harvesters report to Boaz that "since she arrived she has been working hard from this morning until now—except for sitting in the resting hut a short time" (2:7). Later we are told that Ruth worked until evening (v. 17), collecting about thirty pounds of grain. According to Near Eastern culture expert I. J. Gelb, the ration of a male worker in the Old Babylonian period seldom exceeded one to two pounds per day.[10] This would mean that Ruth collected the equivalent of at least half a month's wages in one day![11] While undoubtedly this large quantity testifies to Boaz's generosity, such an amount also shows that this young Moabite widow did not remain idle but actively lived out her commitment to Naomi.

A final demonstration of Ruth's devotion can be found in Boaz's words on the eve of Ruth's proposal for marriage. The member of the clan of Elimelech decrees, "May you be rewarded by the Lord, dear woman! . . . You have not sought to marry one of the young men, whether poor or rich" (3:10). Ruth had opportunities to marry others, but she chose to preserve the heritage of Naomi's family. She could have forsaken Naomi and filled the void of loss and shattered dreams. Instead, the Moabitess forwent a spouse, carefully guarding her heart.

Bending over daily to gather grain in the blistering sun, enduring the ingratitude of the one to whom she has sworn allegiance, withstanding the ridicules of others, and forgoing the advances of men, Ruth stayed true to her word. Despite adversity and time, Ruth did not waver from the initial commitment she made to Naomi. What a contrast to Naomi, who in the wake of shattered dreams and unfulfilled expectations harbored bitterness.

We will discuss in our walk through the life of Nehemiah the importance of fulfilling our commitments, but may Ruth's life remind us of the importance of staying the course despite unmet goals or thwarted passions. May our lives yield the character of one like Ruth—a woman who did not seek personal gratification but sought to be a woman of integrity.

Marked by a Hope Rooted in Faith

Unmet expectations and shattered dreams will often dismantle hope. The promises of tomorrow appear to be directly linked to the truths of today. Hence, in light of the circumstances in Ruth's life, her hope rooted in deep faith proves to be remarkable. Ruth never looked back nor regretted that she had not followed Orpah. Nor did Ruth gaze at herself and fall into despair. Instead, this young widow placed her faith in the Lord and submitted to Him. As Warren Wiersbe aptly remarks, "She looked away from her poverty and focused on his riches. She forgot her fears and rested on his promises."[12]

Ruth's faith in the Lord was verbalized in her declaration to Naomi (1:16–17). Granted these words accompany Ruth's devotion to her mother-in-law, but the underlying element of Ruth's commitment is her allegiance to the God of Israel. In many ways, this Moabitess serves as a feminine counterpart to Abraham. Both characters left their homes, people, and cultures to follow the Lord. Later Jesus will state that to be His disciple one must renounce all family ties for the sake of the kingdom of God (Matt. 8:21–22; 10:37; 19:29). One wonders if Ruth was familiar with such truths as Deuteronomy records: "For the LORD your God is God of gods and Lord of lords, the great, mighty, and awesome God who is unbiased and takes no bribe, who justly treats the orphan and widow, and who loves resident foreigners, giving them food and clothing" (10:17–18). Either way, the placement of her faith reveals the hope that Ruth found to move forward in life.

As believers, we are told not to focus on the disappointments of life but upon Jesus. The writer of Hebrews commands us to keep "our eyes fixed on Jesus, the pioneer and perfecter of our faith" (12:2). So often Christians look to others or even themselves as the solution to their problems. This was Naomi's predicament. Instead of understanding the Lord as part of the solution, she saw Him as part of the problem; instead of turning to Him, she turned away from Him. Jesus sets the model for us. The writer of Hebrews writes, "Think of him who endured such opposition against himself by sinners, so that you may not grow weary in your souls and give up. You have not yet resisted to the point of bloodshed in your struggle against sin" (12:3–4).

Our faith in the Lord yields hope, because Jesus Christ is our hope (1 Tim. 1:1; 1 Thess. 1:3; Col. 1:27). Consequently, Peter can proclaim, "By his great mercy he gave us new birth into a living hope through the resurrection of Jesus Christ from the dead, that is, into an inheritance imperishable, undefiled, and unfading. It is reserved in heaven for you" (1 Peter 1:3b–4). Faith moves our eyes beyond the disappointments of the "here and now" and draws out attention to the hope of the "then and there." We should be cognizant that our hope is not based on a whimsical belief, fanciful prediction, or a blind leap. The surety of our hope is rooted in Jesus Christ's resurrection (see 1 Peter 1:21). We also should observe from Peter's words that the Lord guarantees our hope—it will not dissolve, perish, or fail. Hebrews 11:1 summarizes it well: "Now faith is being *sure* of what we hope for, being *convinced* of what we do not see" (emphasis mine).

Special Dividends and Unique Opportunities

In the midst of her bitterness, Naomi had forgotten the resources she had—her own life, her daughter-in-law, her Lord, and her community. As noted above, Ruth's response to life's disappointments varied drastically from her mother-in-law's. She approached her shattered dreams looking outward, willing to sacrifice personal preferences and remaining devoted to Naomi. Ruth also looked upward as she maintained a hope rooted in her faith in Yahweh. As a result of this Moabite widow's reaction to life's curveballs, she was afforded the opportunity for obedience, the opportunity to experience God's presence and provision, and the opportunity to bless others. Let us examine these three prospects in detail.

An Opportunity for Obedience

At the beginning of the story, Ruth was faced with two different scenarios—either she could return to Moab and pursue her own life or she could follow Naomi and ultimately the Lord. Despite being a young "believer" in the Israelite faith, Ruth understood theologically the privilege and joy that comes from having the opportunity to obey. Her decision to serve the Lord and others rather than herself granted her the reputation of a "worthy" woman (Ruth 3:11).[13] The word for "worthy," *hayil*, appears three times in the description of the virtuous woman in Proverbs 31:10–31. The Word extols the woman for her faithfulness to her social, religious, and domestic responsibilities. Such a character was Ruth. She availed herself of the opportunity to obey.

We need to be careful that we do not miss the wonderful experiences of serving the Lord and others because of disobedience. The great inventor Thomas Edison once said, "Opportunity is missed by most people because it is dressed in overalls and looks like work."[14] At times, obeying the Lord appears more like a burden or a ball and chain. And yet, imagine if the President of the United States called and requested your assistance on his next trip to Europe. Your task consisted of making sure his fountain pen was always full of ink. This meant you would have to travel with him on Air Force One and attend all meetings that he would have with various dignitaries. I dare say the average person would gladly accommodate and even provide the ink. Of obvious greater importance, the Lord of this universe has requested our services. All supplies are provided. We will have direct access to Him and will enjoy His undivided attention at all times. In fact, He is so thrilled to have our assistance that He has made us official members of His family. The question is then, why do we frequently resist serving? That the Lord would even use us should make us grateful. As Paul indicates in his epistle to the church at Philippi, we are to rejoice in serving the Lord (Phil. 4:1, 4). And as the hymn writer says, "to be happy in Jesus" is but "to trust and obey."[15]

An Opportunity to Experience God's Presence and Provision

The Lord does not carry on a conversation with the main character in the book of Ruth as He does with Jeremiah. In fact, the presence of Yahweh through miraculous signs or awesome displays of special revelation is absent in this narrative.[16] Yet the book of Ruth clearly depicts the Lord as the central figure in the story. Eight times the characters speak of God's activities (e.g., 1:13, 20–21; 2:20; 4:12, 14). The narrative also displays a large undertow of God's sovereign hand. His providence can be witnessed in Ruth's "happening" to pick a field that belonged to Boaz (2:3), Boaz's ability to serve as Ruth's kinsman redeemer,[17] and the provision for Elimelech's family (not to mention giving Israel King David).

The Lord can seem so far removed in the midst of shredded dreams. Darkness engulfs one's soul when the Light of the world appears to have dissipated. Ruth could have never imagined the Lord's provisions when she decided to accompany Naomi to the land of Judah. Nor could Ruth have encountered Yahweh's presence and provision had she not experienced failed expectations and crumbled dreams. As witnessed in the narrative, the Lord was not idle, sitting with His arms crossed. Rather, He was actively involved, wrapping His loving arms around Ruth.

Even when it seems that our dreams have, for all practical purposes, died, we can remember this beautiful Old Testament story which reminds us of the Lord's care for us. Some of the darkest hours of life grant the clearest pictures of our Savior. The great hymn writer of a previous century, William Cowper, was subject to clinical depression. Reflecting on those times of deep depression with which he struggled continually, he writes:

> *God moves in a mysterious way*
> *His wonders to perform;*
> *He plants His footsteps in the sea,*
> *And rides upon the storm,*
> *Deep in unfathomable mines*
> *Of never-failing skill*
> *He treasures up His bright designs,*
> *And works His sovereign will.*[18]

If you had asked Ruth upon the death of her husband to explain the ways of the Lord, she would have been speechless. Who would have ever dreamed that a Moabite woman would be the great grandmother of David and a participant in the genealogy of our Savior! We need to be cautious, however, in thinking, "If I stay committed to the Lord and serve others, then He will bless me with what I really want." God does as He pleases (cf. Ps. 115:3; Isa. 45:9; Dan. 4:35), but in so doing He has promised to always be with us and to bless those who seek His face. Joni Eareckson Tada summarizes it well: "We ask less of this life because we know full well that more is coming in the next. The art of living with suffering is just the art of readjusting our expectations in the here and the now."[19] The tragic events of Ruth's life led to blessings beyond imagination—the blessing of abiding in the presence of her Lord and benefiting from the fruits of His hand (Ruth 3:10).

An Opportunity to Bless Others

As we have observed in the book of Ruth, heartbreaks of life can either mold and shape us or they can break us. Bitterness toward those around her, anger at those with spouses and children, and a less-than-inviting demeanor as she labored in the fields could have been Ruth's response to the "misfortunes" of her life. This Moabite widow could have easily reflected the temperament of her mother-in-law—a temperament marked by bitterness toward the Lord and a self-pity that blinded her to the needs of other people. Instead, Ruth's responses to her difficult situation afforded her yet another opportunity—the chance to bless others.

The most obvious and greatest way in which Ruth blessed others was through marrying Boaz and giving birth to a son. Not only did Ruth, through God's grace, provide a guardian for Naomi (4:14), she also rescued Elimelech's family from the tragedy of having no heir. Old Testament scholar, Katharine Doob Sakenfeld summarizes it well:

> The narrative suggests that through the actions of faithful people around her who embody divine faithfulness Naomi is not left in a condition of unrelieved calamity and bitterness. She is offered anew the affection of others, the security of economic survival and of family relationships, and the assurance of care for her time of old age, and she is able to experience these basics of human existence as real and meaningful.[20]

Ruth's obedience not only blessed those immediately around her, but the entire nation of Israel (i.e., David) and ultimately the entire world (i.e., Jesus). One commentator writes, "Like Ruth, Tamar was a foreigner who perpetuated a family line threatened with extinction, one which later became Judah's leading house, and thereby gained herself fame as its founding mother."[21] A faithful follower of Christ will impart blessings that will transcend his or her lifetime. "The book of Ruth affirms that God often effects his purposes in the world through the ordinary motivations and events of his people—ordinary people like Ruth and Boaz, or like you and me, the ripple of whose lives stirs little beyond the pool of their own community—and in particular through their acts of gracious and loving-kindness that go beyond the call of duty."[22]

Conclusion

Disappointed with life's circumstances? Wondering why the life you planned has been dashed to pieces? Why you? Ruth faced the same haunting questions. She could have shaken her fist at God and deserted her mother-in-law. Certainly her mother-in-law provided little to no encouragement in these matters. And yet, thankfully, neither the tragic loss of her husband nor Naomi's bitterness thwarted Ruth.

As we noted in our study of the book, Ruth demonstrated strong determination and unfailing devotion. This was exhibited in three ways. First, her life was marked by an expression of sacrificial love. Despite her own emotional and physical needs, Ruth reached out to Naomi. Second, faithful adherence to a commitment marked the character of Ruth. Her allegiance to Naomi remained constant regardless of how turbulent life appeared. Finally, Ruth displayed a hope rooted in faith. Her eyes were not only directed horizontally as she provided for her mother-in-law, but also vertically, as she looked to Yahweh as a source of strength and hope. As a result, Ruth benefited from three great blessings—the opportunity for obedience, the opportunity to experience God's presence and provision, and the opportunity to bless others.

For Reflection

1. Are you currently facing one of life's unmet expectations or shattered dreams? If so, how are you addressing the opportunities of obeying, experiencing the Lord's presence and provision, and blessing others?
2. When Boaz met Ruth, he may have been past the age when most Jewish men married. Hence, he would have encountered social stigma. Reread the book of Ruth observing how Boaz

demonstrated "loyal love" (*ḥesed*) despite his circumstances. Be sure to note his respect for Ruth and integrity the night she came to him to propose marriage.

3. As you reflect upon this small but powerful book, think of someone who has served as a "Ruth" in your life when you faced a difficulty? Be sure to express your gratitude for that person's role in your life.

6

Joseph
Purity in the Midst of Temptation

Men's favor is worth very little after all, in comparison with the favor of Christ.
> —J. Gresham Machen, 1881–1937
> (single man who founded and
> served as first president of Westminster
> Theological Seminary, Philadelphia)

The story was told of a fellow who was driving home late one night when he picked up a hitchhiker. As they rode along, he began to be suspicious of his passenger. The fellow checked to see if his wallet was safe in the pocket of his coat that was on the seat between them, but it was not there! So he slammed on the brakes, and ordered the hitchhiker out of the car. He then shouted, "Hand over the wallet immediately!" The frightened traveler handed over a billfold, and the fellow drove off. When he arrived home, he started to tell his wife about the experience, but she interrupted him, saying, "Before I forget, do you know that you left your wallet at home this morning?"[1]

Like this unfortunate traveler, singles often fall victim to the suspicions of others. Besides implied accusations of "social inadequacies" looms the assumption that a single is more prone to sexual failure. Many churches will not consider hiring a single adult for this reason. Some married adults go beyond this assumption and also assume single adults actually *are* sexually promiscuous. When these faulty beliefs are verbalized, they only compound the pain singles can face.

Unfortunately, not all of these suspicions are unfounded. Immorality does plague many singles. For instance, a recent Barna study showed that 52 percent of single adults versus 36 percent of married adults believe reading a magazine with explicit sexual pictures or nudity is morally acceptable; 67 percent of never-been-married adults versus 45 percent of married adults believe watching a movie with explicit sex or nudity is morally acceptable.[2] Many singles and married adults also hold different opinions concerning cohabitation and homosexuality.

Rather than examining the entire life of Joseph, we will explore only one episode. In Genesis 37, Potiphar, the captain of the guard for Pharaoh, purchases Joseph as a slave. Potiphar's wife attempts to seduce Joseph, fails, and then accuses him of attacking her (Gen. 39). Throughout the centuries, this story of Joseph has served as a paradigm for temperance and chastity.[3] We will study the characteristics of temptation and its devastating effects. Then we will see from Genesis 39 how Joseph stood strong despite his master's wife's lies and false charges. Single adults must not only escape the pitfalls of temptation, they must also be able to refute hasty accusations.

Joseph: A Single Man in the Face of Temptation

Temptation has been defined as "an allurement or enticement to do evil . . . a trap into which the unwary can fall (1 Tim. 6:9) . . . the state of being tempted to do evil."[4] Joseph's encounter with his master's wife provides the perfect case study, and from it we can glean four important points concerning how allurement operates. The account of this favorite son of Jacob also displays the necessity of an acute awareness of sin and the value of possessing a heart fixed upon the Lord.

The Need to Understand Temptation

Temptation grants no exemptions. Even the Son of God was tempted when He walked this earth (see Heb. 4:15). Age will not disqualify you. Gender, race, and marital status will not bestow on you any advantages. Nor will your education or social status eliminate you.

No matter who you are, temptation will find you. Pastor and author Richard Exley writes in his recent book on spiritual resources for avoiding temptation and its consequences:

> We shouldn't really be surprised when we are accosted by sinful desires, regardless of the form they may take. No matter how spiritually mature we become, we will never escape the reach of temptation. Being tempted is not a sign of carnality as much as it is evidence of our humanity. On this fallen planet temptation is a fact of life![5]

While temptation's tactics will vary from person to person, its visitation will not.[6] Jesus recognized these matters surrounding temptation when He taught us to pray "lead us not into temptation" (see Matt. 6:13).

Because of temptation's impartiality, we can glean some valuable insights from Joseph. Although he lived thousands of years ago, the life of this single Hebrew male is relevant today. "Indeed," writes Cornelius Plantinga Jr. in his preface to *Not the Way It's Supposed to Be: A Breviary of Sin*, "for most of us a healthy reminder of our sin and guilt allows hope. . . . What we need periodically are presentations of main themes that arise within the traditional Christian understanding of sin."[7] I could not agree more. A more astute understanding of the enemy will assist in our spiritual battles.

Regardless of our marital status, temptation—whether it is indulging in sexual pleasures, trusting externals to satisfy, idolizing food, or filling our lives with the trivial—confronts each of us. Exposing the enemy's tactics and recognizing our own weaknesses will assist in our pursuit of holy living. From the life of Joseph, let us explore four ways temptation frequently functions.

A Product of the Opportune Moment

At twenty-seven years of age, Joseph was alone in a foreign country. His solo living did not originate from a study abroad program or a stint with the Red Cross; Joseph was alone because his brothers betrayed him and sold him into slavery. An Egyptian administrator by the name of Potiphar purchased the Hebrew slave. Through a series of events, Joseph secured the position of managing his master's immediate household.[8] Here Joseph, described in Genesis 39:6 as "well built and good looking," found himself frequently in the presence of his master's wife. To complicate matters, Potiphar's business entailed numerous road trips. A victim of a dysfunctional home with his future hanging in the balance, Joseph's hurting soul lay exposed and vulnerable.

The first lesson Genesis 39 teaches us is that temptation waits for the opportune moment. Potiphar's wife had carefully schemed the entire situation. Waiting, she sought the perfect chance to be alone with Joseph. Verse 11 clearly indicates such: "One day he went into the house to do his work, when none of the household servants were there in the house. She grabbed him by his outer garment . . ." (vv. 11–12a). You can almost hear Potiphar's wife: "No one will know. We are all alone. Potiphar would never suspect."

Temptation seems omniscient, waiting for a period of greatest vulnerability. Noting this fact, the apostle Paul warns, "So let the one who thinks he is standing be careful that he does not fall" (1 Cor. 10:12).

Drawing a vivid picture of Satan, the apostle Peter warns his readers: "Discipline yourselves, keep alert. Like a roaring lion your adversary the devil prowls around, looking for someone to devour" (1 Peter 5:8 NRSV). This verse makes me think of flannelgraph lessons in Sunday school when my teacher would put up a picture of a prowling lion and warn us about Satan, the one who chases us down and destroys us if we are not on guard. And yet, was I ever surprised recently to learn that lions are not particularly efficient hunters. They are not well suited for running high speeds or long distances, and thus will stop chasing their prey after a few yards. They are, however, well suited for catching prey at short distances. Often with one giant leap, the lion will topple its prey and bite its neck—either underneath in order to strangle it or above to sever the spinal chord. Lions prefer to hunt at night when their light-gathering eyes give them a distinct advantage.[9] Peter's call for discipline and alertness is all the more urgent given these characteristics of a lion.[10] Satan's attack will seldom, if ever, be frontal. Instead he lurks in the shadow waiting for the moment when we least expect it. Also, note that when the attack is made, there is little escape for the prey. The person who fails to be on guard will most likely be destroyed.

A Potential Companion of Success

One of Satan's most opportune times to tempt us is in the wake of success. Temptation often waits in the shadows during a spiritual victory, physical accomplishment, or emotional high. Puritan pastor and theologian John Owen writes in his classic book, *Sin and Temptation:*

> Temptation makes every profession and vocation a potential snare. Some find themselves the darlings, the celebrities, the popular ones in their own circle of friends and associates. Once these thoughts enter into their hearts, temptation entangles them. Instead of seeking to gain more glory, they need to lie in the dust, out of a sense of the vileness in themselves.[11]

Solomon, in his great wisdom, also observes, "The prosperity of fools shall destroy them" (Prov. 1:32b KJV).

From the pit near Shechem to a governor's mansion in Egypt, Joseph undoubtedly reveled in the fortunate turn of events as he took his position of authority. Five times the text indicates there was a blessing upon all that Joseph did and received. Furthermore, twice the text speaks of the Lord's blessing upon Potiphar because of the presence of this twenty-seven-year-old. The danger for Joseph in his prestigious role was overlooking the grace of God. In *Joseph: A Man of Integrity and Forgiveness,* Charles Swindoll addresses the danger of temptation: "You must not be weakened by your situation, you must not be deceived by the persuasion, you must be gentle with your emotions, you must not be confused with the immediate results."[12] How easy it probably was for Joseph to call upon the Lord as he was cast into the pit. However, it could have been just as easy for Joseph to forget the Lord during his life of comfort and success in Potiphar's home. In his thought-provoking work on the life of Joseph, Bible teacher F. B. Meyer warns:

> We may expect temptation in the days of prosperity and ease rather than in those of privation and toil.

Not on the glacier slopes of the Alps, but in the sunny plains of Campagna; not when the youth is climbing arduously the steep ladder of fame, but when he has entered the golden portals; not where men frown, but where they smile sweet exquisite smiles of flattery—it is there, it is there, that the temptress lies in wait! Beware![13]

Success, good health, and wealth can rob us of our dependence upon the Lord and dull our senses to the dangers of temptation.

Temptation's partnership with life's triumphs can also be witnessed in the lives of various biblical characters: Noah's drunkenness after the flood; Lot's sexual relations with his daughters directly following his deliverance from Sodom and Gomorrah; David's affair with Bathsheba after numerous military successes; Elijah's period of loneliness and depression succeeding his victory at Mount Carmel; and Peter's rebuke after his strong christological declaration. If Joseph and these other biblical figures tell us anything, they warn us to take heed. May the words concerning Moses in Hebrews 11:24–26 be ascribed to us: "By faith, when he grew up, Moses refused to be called the son of Pharaoh's daughter, choosing rather to be ill-treated with the people of God than to enjoy sin's fleeting pleasure. He regarded abuse suffered for Christ to be greater wealth than the treasures of Egypt, for his eyes were fixed on the reward."

A Relentless Pursuit

Recently, I incurred health issues from the consumption of coffee . . . in large quantities. Through a series of negotiations, my doctor consented to allow the ingestion of this nectar in decaffeinated form. My adherence to the doctor's orders was impeccable, until day two. That morning our office's stockpile of unleaded coffee was exhausted. I resisted. Later that morning, a colleague and I visited a coffee shop. The "brew of the day" was my favorite blend . . . caffeinated, of course. Again, I resisted. During lunch, my friend went and grabbed us both a cup of coffee. It, too, was caffeinated. It seemed that everywhere I turned, I was faced with the choice of continuing this decaffeinated exile or surrendering. While I withstood the first two tests, I waved the white flag and subjected my body to the cup of coffee delivered by my friend.

Temptation functions in a similar manner. The allure is seldom, if ever, a one-time event. Rather, it is frequently delivered, wearing down our guard. Genesis 39:10 tells us that "even though she continued to speak to Joseph day after day, he did not respond to her invitation to have sex with her." Potiphar's wife did not just entice Joseph once, but obsessively persisted in seeking to have a sexual encounter with him. In fact, the frankness of her words and her later aggression (displayed by grabbing his clothing) demonstrates the ongoing threat she presented. Her actions also demonstrate an increase in the intensity with which she approached Joseph. When a believer succumbs to temptation, it is seldom a sudden event. Underlying the collapse is a foundation worn down over time. Later in this chapter we will discuss ways to shore up the foundation stones and ensure that they withstand whatever might come.

A Potential for Adverse Results if Rejected

Imagine if Joseph had consented to Potiphar's wife's wishes. The wake of destruction stemming from his sin would have affected Potiphar, Potiphar's wife, Joseph, and ultimately his family. First, Joseph would have severed the trust and privileges obtained through his position, borne the weight of guilt within his own soul, and possibly even been sentenced to death for committing such an act in Egypt.[14] However, even if the infidelity had gone undetected and his conscience had gone unseared, Joseph probably would have never met Pharaoh's cupbearer. This acquaintance led Joseph to serving as the overseer of Pharaoh's household and the administrator of the food that fed not only Egypt, but Israel, during the seven-year famine.

And yet, refusing to accept temptation's call does not necessarily mean we will enter "a land flowing with milk and honey." Resisting temptation can be costly. Although God did not forsake Joseph, the decision to run rather than relax with Potiphar's wife bore seemingly adverse consequences. First, Joseph faced the harsh and deceitful slander of his master's wife. His faithfulness and purity were made suspect by the words "That Hebrew slave you brought to us tried to humiliate me, but when I raised my voice and screamed, he left his outer garment and ran outside" (39:17–18). Old Testament scholar Victor Hamilton explains the significance of this episode: "The charge is deliberate. To be sexually attacked is bad enough. To be sexually attacked by a foreign slave makes her accusation all the more damning. In choosing this term, she is putting Joseph in as despicable a light as possible."[15] Note also that Potiphar's wife omitted the phrase "beside me" or the actual details of the event in which Joseph "left his outer garment in her hand" when relaying the scene to her husband so as to distance herself and thus remove any implications of her guilt. Her venomous words undoubtedly paralyzed Joseph.

Another adverse side effect of resisting temptation was Joseph's banishment from the comforts of Potiphar's household to "the place where the king's prisoners were confined" (v. 20). Joseph's reward for devotion to his master was incarceration. Nevertheless, several Bible scholars propose that Potiphar believed Joseph. John Walton wrote these words in his commentary on Genesis, "Given his wife's slander of his own motives, the proven trustworthiness of Joseph, the fact that he is going to lose the services of a competent slave, and his knowledge of his wife's character or lack of it, his anger arguably burns at his wife, not at Joseph."[16] That Potiphar let Joseph live further supports the claim that he questioned the accuracy of his wife's testimony.[17] And yet, even if Potiphar suspected Joseph's innocence, actions must be taken to save face. Joseph must be sentenced.

A prevalent view among evangelicals suggests that obedience warrants blessing. We assume that the Lord owes us something for our devotion and commitment not to surrender to temptation. However, God never promised His children ease and comfort in this life. If His own Son hung on a tree because He yielded to His Father's will, why should we expect anything less?

Summary

While we could explore further characteristics of temptation, Genesis 39 illustrates the picture clearly and serves as a solid base from which to understand how sin presents itself to us. It waits for the opportune moment—often accompanying success—relentlessly pursues us, and creates the potential for adversity if it is rejected.

The Need for a Healthy Understanding of Sin

Understanding the characteristics of temptation is key to withstanding its lure. In addition, we must also grasp the magnitude of sin. Joseph's response to his master's wife reveals his healthy comprehension of the seriousness of immorality. He refuses, saying, "Look, my master does not give any thought to his household with me here, and everything that he owns he has put into my care. There is no one greater in this household than I am. He has withheld nothing from me except you because you are his wife. So how could I do such a great evil and sin against God?" (vv. 8–9). We have already briefly addressed the potential ramifications if Joseph had committed adultery, but apart from the effects on people around him and himself, Joseph notes that the ultimate offense is against God. James Montgomery Boice paraphrases Joseph's words, "How could I—I who have known the true God and have been the beneficiary of his grace, I who have been taught the difference between right and wrong, I who have been redeemed from sin by the precious blood of Jesus Christ—how could I do such a wicked thing and sin against God?"[18] Sin is a personal affront to a personal God. Plantinga comments, "Sin is not only the breaking of law but also the breaking of a covenant with one's savior. Sin is the smearing of a relationship, the grieving of one's divine parent and benefactor, a betrayal of the partner to whom one is joined by a holy bond."[19] King David recognizes this in his confession to the Lord after his affair with Bathsheba. He declares, "For I am aware of my rebellious acts; I am forever conscious of my sin. Against you, especially you, I have sinned" (Ps. 51:3–4a). May we constantly remember that sin is enmity with the Lord (see Gal. 5:17) and is an aversion to Him (see Eph. 2:1–3).

Frequently, when counseling students who convey no remorse for or rejection of sinful behavior, I hear, "I can handle this"; "God wants me to be happy"; or "You just don't understand my situation." Betrayed by his own family, sold into slavery, robbed of the pursuit of a spouse in his early twenties, and alone in a foreign country, Joseph could have easily leveled any one of these excuses. However, Joseph's concern focused upon the Lord rather than himself. James recognizes the heart of our sin. He writes:

> Let no one say when he is tempted, "I am tempted
> by God," for God cannot be tempted by evil, and
> he himself tempts no one. But each one is tempted
> when he is lured and enticed by his own desires.
> Then when desire conceives, it gives birth to sin.
> (James 1:13–15)

The root of our treachery is not the Lord nor Satan; rather, it lies within our very own hearts (see, e.g., Rom. 7:18). Our wants become needs, the self replaces service, and our lives become engrossed in living out our own passions. In David Wells's excellent but disturbing assessment of present culture, he reflects,

> Theology becomes therapy . . . the biblical interest in
> righteousness is replaced by a search for happiness,
> holiness by wholeness, truth by feeling, ethics by feel-
> ing good about one's self. The world shrinks to the
> range of personal circumstances; the community of
> faith shrinks to a circle of personal friends. The past
> recedes. The Church recedes. The world recedes. All
> that remains is the self.[20]

Sin calls for allegiance to self rather than to the Savior, pleading for us to save our own lives and knowing that such actions will only result in the forfeit of our souls (see Mark 8:35).[21]

Joseph's actions, as well as his words, display his abhorrence of sin. Four times we are told in Genesis 39 that this single man left his outer garment and ran outside. Joseph did not stay long enough for Potiphar's wife to remove any further clothing, nor did he run to another part of the house. He completely left the premises. Cornelius Plantinga Jr. aptly cautions, "Nobody studies sin very long without discovering that the subject is full of depths, turns, ironies, and surprises."[22] If we comprehended the danger of sin, we would not entertain it, let alone make provision for it. If doctors discovered a malignant tumor in your thyroid gland, they would not tell you to go home and ignore the issue. Rather, they would remove not only the tumor but also much of the organ. They would then probably follow up with radiation treatment and regular checkups. Sin bears far worse consequences than cancer. Hence, it calls for radical treatment and drastic measures for eradication. Facing temptation calls for proactive behavior. The German theologian Jürgen Moltmann writes,

> To be sure, it is usually said that sin in its original form is man's wanting to be as God. But that is only the one side of sin. The other side of such pride is hopelessness, resignation, inertia and melancholy. . . . Temptation then consists not so much in the titanic desire to be as God, but in weakness, timidity, weariness, not wanting to be what God requires of us.[23]

Allowing the cancer of sin to continue ultimately leads to death (James 1:15).

The Need for a Heart Fixed upon the Lord

A final component necessary in the midst of temptation is a heart fixed upon the Lord. The apostle John cautions his readers not to love the world or the things in the world, advising that they should set their affection on things above (1 John 2:15–17; cf. Ps. 57). The heart that cherishes the things of God will immerse itself in the worship of Him. Such activity will expose the frauds of life and will be dissatisfied with any substitute (e.g., relationships, possessions, occupations).

A heart that is in tune with the Lord finds nourishment from three sources. The first essential to the spiritual walk is prayer. While we could say much on this topic, John Owen provides four key insights on the value of prayer in relationship to temptation.[24] First, prayer reveals all the secret workings and actions of sin, calling attention to our soul's needs, frustrations, and predicaments. Frequently, David would pour out his soul in complaint before the Lord (e.g., Ps. 102). The second value of prayer concerns its effect on the heart. Prayer pierces the heart, exposing the vileness of sin. The third point observed by John Owen is that prayer provides the means to obtain strength and power against sin. The writer of Hebrews assures that we will find help in time of need (4:16), and James commands us to ask of the Lord during our trials (1:5). Paul reminds us that the

Lord is ready to assist when we need Him. The apostle informs us that "no trial has overtaken you that is not faced by others. And God is faithful: He will not let you be tried beyond what you are able to bear, but with the trial will also provide a way out so that you may be able to endure it" (1 Cor. 10:13). It is the Lord who knows how to deliver the godly out of temptation (2 Peter 2:9). The Lord may deliver you, alter the source of your temptation, tread down Satan, provide a source of grace, provide an assurance of success, or utterly remove the temptation; but you can successfully stand with His help. Finally, prayer counteracts all the deceitful workings of sin by drawing us into the presence of the Lord, purifying our longings, and attuning our passions.

The soul also finds nourishment from meditation and study of God's Word. Psalm 119:9–10 reads, "How can a young person maintain a pure lifestyle? By following your instructions! With all my heart I seek you. Do not allow me to stray from your commands!" Later in the psalm, the writer proclaims:

> Your words are tastier in my mouth than honey! Your precepts give me discernment. Therefore I hate all deceitful actions. Your instructions are a lamp that shows me where to walk, and a light that shines on my path. I have vowed and solemnly sworn to keep your just regulations. (vv. 103–106)

The Lord communicates with us through the Bible. Danger arises when we attempt to remove ourselves from His instruction. People's disregard for the Word of God has provided the breeding ground for the epidemic of spiritual atrophy we face today. Instead of turning to the Lord's words as the basis for our moral and ethical decisions, one out of every four single adults turns to what feels right or what is most comfortable in a situation.[25] In fact, only 10 percent of single adults, versus 22 percent of married adults, base moral and ethical decisions on the Bible.[26] George Barna aptly writes:

> Four times as many widowed adults are as likely to say that abortion is morally acceptable as they are to say that getting drunk is acceptable. Divorced adults

> are more likely to condone pornography, homosexuality and cohabitation than drunkenness. The never-been-married folks in our nation are more prone to endorse pornography, cohabitation, abortion and homosexuality than to support drunkenness or stealing. . . . And the reasoning is simple: Lacking any moral standard as a basis for such considerations, the final determination of right and wrong is personal and conditional. The result is an unusual and unpredictable scrabble of values and behaviors.[27]

Without the inspired Word of God, we are left with no useful and effective tool for teaching, for reproof, for correction, and for training in righteousness. It is the only means for a man or woman to be capable and equipped for every good work (2 Tim. 3:16–17).

Not only do prayer and God's Word facilitate our defense against the onslaught of temptation, but the community of God is also part of a powerful defense. Sharing our deepest struggles weakens any design temptation may have upon us. The interaction and exposure release us from the need to pretend and open the floodgates of intercessory prayer. Galatians 6:2 calls for believers to bear one another's burdens in order to fulfill the law of Christ. We need to submit ourselves to a local body of believers and, if possible, to an accountability partner. In sharing with our brothers and sisters in Christ we find acceptance, support, encouragement, and, when needed, forgiveness.

Joseph: A Single Man in the Face of False Accusations

Perhaps your life resonates with Joseph's. You have successfully withstood the temptation, but the aftermath of accusations has taken its toll. Bearing the gift of singleness and maintaining purity is difficult enough, let alone having rumors fly that you have a loose lifestyle or that your sexual orientation is questionable. How did Joseph continue to serve the Lord despite the venomous slander of his master's wife and the subsequent imprisonment? A careful look at Genesis 39 reveals two significant aspects of Joseph's perseverance that are essential to surviving the onslaught of hurtful accusations and slander.

The Recognition of the Lord's Presence

The idea reverberates through the chapter that "The LORD was with Joseph." Reminiscent of the earlier patriarchs (Gen. 26:3; 28:15; 31:3), our author records God's presence as a fact. Victor Hamilton so poignantly remarks,

> The name Yahweh occurs here at what is the most uncertain moment in the life of Joseph. His future hangs in the balance. He is alone in Egypt, separated from family, vulnerable, with a cloud over his future. Or is he alone? Only the narrator, never any of the characters, uses the name Yahweh. Thus, it is the narrator who tells us, no less than five times, that in a very precarious situation, Joseph is not really alone. Yahweh is with him.[28]

There can be no question. Potiphar recognized it (39:3). The keeper of the prison observed it (39:21). The Lord was with this young Hebrew.

This reality for Joseph was not exclusive but rings throughout the Scriptures as a truth for all of God's people. Having witnessed the Lord's hand forty years, Moses shares some parting words to those he has led. One can only imagine not a dry eye was in that gathered group as they heard their revered leader assure them: "Be strong and courageous! Do not fear or tremble before them, for the LORD your God is the one who is going with you. He will not fail you or abandon you! . . . The LORD is indeed going before you—he will be with you; he will not fail you or abandon you. Do not be afraid or discouraged!" (Deut. 31:6–8). So profound and comforting are these words that the writer of Hebrews recalls them as he reminds believers in Christ that the Lord is their helper, and He will not forsake them (Heb. 13:5–6). Regardless of what malicious comments are made concerning us, privately or openly, we can rest in the assurance that our Lord knows and He promises to be by our side.

The Recognition of the Lord's Sovereignty

Intertwined with the Lord's promise of ongoing presence is the reality that He is in control. Potiphar's wife may have thought she stripped Joseph of any future as she held his outer garment in her hands, yet she only facilitated the Lord's design for Joseph's life. During his time in prison, Joseph gained further experience in management; he was once again placed in a position of authority (cf. 39:6, 8, 22). Prison also afforded Joseph the opportunity to meet Pharaoh's butler. Finally, Joseph's imprisonment allowed this single adult to gain further knowledge of God's grace and hand of provision. The prospect of prison after managing a wealthy Egyptian's estate would have been devastating enough, but I dare say the hurled insults and false accusations leveled by his master's wife must have pierced Joseph's very soul. The question of whether it was worth it may have swelled within him. And yet, as Scottish preacher George Lawson aptly stated nearly two hundred years ago,

> It was not Joseph's death, but his imprisonment, that was to be the means of his elevation; and Potiphar, and even Potiphar's wife, served Providence in all the evil which they did to Joseph; whilst they were most egregiously violating His commandments, they were fulfilling His counsels. Let not God's people be afraid of the violence of their enemies. What can man do against God? Not only the righteous and the wise, and their works, but the unrighteous, the unwise, and the worst of their works, are in the hand of God.[29]

One of my greatest struggles in living solo is coping with hurtful comments and innuendos while attempting to walk righteously before my Lord. The life of Joseph reminds me that I suffer from myopia. When the prisons of life come, I can easily miss the Lord's providence. God provided for Paul, John, Samson, Jeremiah, and yes, even Joseph, during their times of incarceration. Aleksandr Solzhenitsyn confesses in an account of his punishment in the Gulag:

> In the intoxication of youthful successes I had felt myself to be infallible, and I was therefore cruel. In

the surfeit of power I was a murderer, and an oppressor. In my most evil moments I was convinced that I was doing good, and I was well supplied with systematic arguments. And it was only when I lay there on rotting prison straw that I sensed within myself the first stirrings of good. Gradually, it was disclosed to me that the line separating good and evil passes not through states, not between classes, not between political parties either—but right through every human heart—and through all human hearts. . . . So bless you, prison, for having been in my life.[30]

Conclusion

While the time, place, and people may vastly differ from our world, the issues surrounding temptation in Genesis 39 remain constant. Through the life of Joseph we observe the need to understand the various traits of temptation, to recognize the destruction of sin, and to grow in our affection for the Lord. We witnessed a man who for many reasons could have easily succumbed to sexual temptation, yet was able to remain faithful to the God of Israel. Unfortunately, we also noted that resisting temptation will not necessarily win the praise of all people. Like many single adults who attempt to live for the Lord, Joseph became the focal point of verbal attack. Instead of becoming bitter or retaliating against the false accusations and questions concerning his fidelity, Joseph rested in the Lord's promises and in His sovereignty.

For Reflection

1. Given all of the circumstances of your life—community, workplace, school, home—what would make other people look at your life and say, "The Lord is certainly with that person"?
2. Contrast the incident of Joseph and Potiphar's wife with the story of David and Bathsheba in 2 Samuel 11–12. What are the most important lessons this scene from the life of David has for us today?
3. In what area of your Christian walk do you feel most secure?

Take time to immediately ask for God's grace in this area of your life and commit it anew to Him.

4. How different do you think your life could be if you were to identify one key behavior you would like to change and then submit it to God daily?

7

Nehemiah

Not Going "A-Wall" (AWOL)

> Jesus knows we're gonna fall. He knew it before He
> created us. And He doesn't want our failure to throw
> us. . . . Our focus shouldn't be on our failure, but on
> our Father. You may stumble and fall, but trust in
> God and don't let it throw you.
>
> —Mark Lowry
> (a never-been-married comedian and Southern Gospel singer)

"I have had it! I am tired of trying to minister to singles at our church. They are too independent and unreliable. They cannot commit to a single event, let alone to the church!" bemoaned the disgruntled pastor after Friday's poorly attended social event. Though I wish this were an isolated statement, numerous ministers and church workers are expressing similar complaints. While single adults indicate that the greatest issue they face is loneliness, most married individuals believe the number one problem for singles is commitment. Just the word *commitment* can send a shock wave that registers on the seismograph of some single adults. The fault lines appear in relationships, involvement in church, and even in private lives.

My words might appear harsh and unfounded so let me offer a few disclaimers. First, I am not talking about the reason why some singles are reluctant to "tie the knot." While we could, and probably should, speak to the individual who has not yet married despite dating the same person for more than thirty years, our topic encompasses a far broader issue. Secondly, I recognize that we are stereotyping. Many singles display a character of devotion. A third disclaimer acknowledges that the lack of domestic responsibilities and the variety of interests that come from living solo may *appear* as unfaithfulness and irresponsibility, when in reality, single people are usually very busy. And finally, the appearance of disloyalty may simply be a single adult's knee-jerk reaction to the way he or she has been treated in the church or by individuals. Being segregated into a Sunday school class that looks like an extended youth group and that is tucked away in a musty room in the church basement does not foster a sense of belonging or a desire to belong.

And yet, despite all of these disclaimers, let us be realistic. One is hard pressed to find a thriving singles group with faithful attendance and heavy involvement in the local church. Anyone who has been involved in ministering to singles knows the frustration expressed above by the pastor. Herding a group of cats can be easier than organizing a social event for unmarrieds. In addition, studies show that marriage and the presence of young children yield a higher probability of church attendance.[1] In George Barna's recent research he confesses,

> Single adults are not an easy group to understand. And it is often because they do not understand (or accept) themselves and their present state of being. They are influenced by a variety of sources, making it hard to derive a black-and-white picture of who they are, what they think and how they behave. As was noted earlier, increasing numbers of Americans are comfortable with contradictions, even when the paradox in question relates to their own behavior![2]

Hence, while we may not want to admit it, commitment can be hard to find in some single adults.

A biblical character who exemplifies a life of commitment is Nehemiah, the cupbearer of the Persian ruler Artaxerxes I Longiamnus.

Such a position indicates that Nehemiah was trustworthy, well trained in court etiquette, handsome (cf. Dan. 1:4, 13, 15), and probably single.[3] Expert in ancient Near Eastern culture Edwin Yamauchi notes that the cupbearer would have been "a man of great influence as one with closest access to the king, and one who could well determine who got to see the king. Above all Nehemiah would have enjoyed the unreserved confidence of the king."[4] In a turn of events, Artaxerxes I grants Nehemiah permission to return to Jerusalem to rebuild the walls (Neh. 2:1–10). Neither a priest nor a prophet, Nehemiah returns to the land of his forefathers, fulfills his assignment, and serves as the governor of Judah for twelve years. An ancient Jewish writing reflects, "The memory of Nehemiah also is lasting; He raised for us the walls that had fallen, and set up gates and bars and rebuilt our ruined houses" (Sir 49.13).

From servant to political leader, the story of Nehemiah might appear to be Jewish legend—sterilized from any hardships to create a heroic figure for Jewish boys to emulate. However, upon closer examination we quickly realize that Nehemiah's decision to tackle this assignment was far from glorious and led to numerous obstacles. These hurdles bear much resemblance to ones we face in our own lives. The first part of this chapter will investigate the numerous difficulties Nehemiah encountered. We will then explore the means that allowed Nehemiah not only to rebuild the wall, but restore regular temple worship and instruction from God's law, instill Sabbath keeping, and encourage godly family life.

The Hazards of Constructing a Wall

Whether it is the quarterback throwing a pass or the artist painting a portrait, the expert can make the task appear easy and effortless. What we miss are the countless hours of practice, the numerous failures and frustrations, and the enormous sacrifices that were made to reach a place of proficiency. Thankfully, the book of Nehemiah provides greater detail than merely stating that Nehemiah oversaw a building project. We gain a clear understanding of exactly what it cost Nehemiah to oversee the restoration of a wall that was nearly one mile in circuit, three to four feet thick, and fifteen to twenty feet high. The price of his commitment was ridicule, depression, loss of vision, and self-sufficiency. Despite all of these, he remained faithful to his God and to his mission.

The Stones of Ridicule

Nehemiah's decision to rebuild the wall created great opposition, because the rebuilding of the city's wall ensured a presence for the Jews in the region and granted safety from their hostile neighbors—Samaritans to the north, Ammonites to the east, Arabs and Edomites to the south, and Phoenicians to the west.[5] Consequently, foreign opposition was persistent and great as foreign leaders attempted to disrupt Israel's restoration project. Nehemiah tells us that Tobiah, a principal opponent and high-ranking Persian official, sent him letters in order to scare him (6:19). This political albatross delivered not one or two but numerous pieces of "hate mail" in order to wear down the governor's resistance. We also discover that those who opposed Nehemiah developed political alliances (4:7–8) and even hired people to scare him (6:12–13). The Jewish historian Josephus tells that Nehemiah's opponents also "killed many of the Jews and sought to make an end of Nehemiah himself by hiring some foreigners to do away with him."[6] Nehemiah's enemies carefully selected targets for their attacks. While the text never mentions Nehemiah's enemies ridiculing him for his marital status, they did mock him (2:19; 6:6), his workers (4:1–2), his materials (4:2), and his work (4:3). Effective ridicule, the kind that immobilizes a person, is frequent and measures large in intensity.

Contrary to the old saying, "Sticks and stones may break my bones, but names can never hurt me," verbal onslaught and even thoughtless comments from well-meaning people can weaken the very foundation of our commitment. Having the "hello, I'm single" sticker on the forehead seems to provide the perfect target. Several years ago I served on the pastoral staff of a small church. The congregation may not have been large, but their problems were. While certainly not every difficulty was directly related to my ministry, I struggled with my own shortcomings. Those issues were only intensified by a comment from a deacon's wife. I am uncertain to this very day whether she meant it as a compliment when she applauded my role in the church but then proceeded to say how much more wonderful it would be if I had a "helpmate." Already feeling inadequate, the words pierced right through my heart and destroyed my weakening commitment to the ministry there. Shortly after her comments, I resigned from my position.

The Cracks of Depression

One of the reasons ridicule can be so effective is because it causes us to question the veracity of the poisonous words. Thoughts of "I know that if I were married I could better minister to parents" or "Perhaps my singleness is hindering the ministry of this church" haunt our inner beings. Similar cracks of discouragement and depression could have easily appeared in Nehemiah's undertaking. First, the city walls had lain in devastation since the time of the Babylonians. Old Testament scholar and former president of Dallas Theological Seminary Donald Campbell asks an astute question in his book on Nehemiah: "If the report of the Jewish travelers moved him to tears . . . , what must have been the effect of seeing the dismal desolation of Jerusalem with his own eyes?"[7] Complicating matters were Nehemiah's inexperience, a lack of supplies, safety issues, and political opposition. Nehemiah's assignment is comparable to preparing a motley crew of men to play in the Super Bowl when they have never even played a football game, you have to borrow the equipment, and you do not have enough padding for all of the uniforms.

Not too long ago I attended a small singles' gathering where we simply sat around and engaged in small talk. Discussions of the weather and politics were suddenly interrupted by one of my friends, releasing his pent-up frustrations. He blurted, "I am tired of being committed to the Lord, committed to purity, and committed to the church. What use is it? I have nothing to show for it. No spouse. No family. Only a designated place among the social outcasts!" Stunned, we sat in complete silence that lasted for what seemed to be at least ten minutes. Our initial reaction relegated his comment to the realm of heresy, but when he awkwardly attempted to recant, to my amazement, several others began expressing similar struggles. The chain reaction triggered by my friend's words made me wonder if I had stumbled into a "lack of devotion" anonymous group. The events of that evening provided a clear picture of the potential effects discouragement and depression can have on commitment. This diabolical duo can not only prevent commitment; they can destroy a person's life.

The Loss of Vision

The loss of vision can also have an adverse effect on commitment. While Nehemiah had little problem motivating the people, sustaining this motivation through completion of the project would have been extremely difficult in the midst of the ridicule and discouragement. The text tells us that the Jews complained, "The strength of the laborers has failed! The debris is so great that we are unable to rebuild the wall" (4:10). In addition, Nehemiah himself acknowledges that the work was demanding and extensive (4:19). He could have easily left the construction site or in frustration done a halfhearted job so he could return home. Devotion to a cause can only be as strong as the clarity of the goal.

Two years ago I created the perfect fitness plan. I had read the book, obtained the supplements, and laid out a dietary schedule. In twelve weeks I would transform my body into a lean machine . . . at least this is what *Body for Life* implied. My enthusiasm for this "life-changing" endeavor was so great that I made the fatal error of sharing my plan with several friends. Instead of expressions of joy, snide comments such as "You have to be joking" and "I bet you will not last for a week" were made. Then came the protein shakes. I can still taste the chalky paste as it slowly slid down my throat. There was definitely no need to fear a fiber deficiency. These various obstacles blocked my vision of a washboard chest, and my attention turned to what appeared as insurmountable hurdles. As a result, I lost sight of the goal. Our mission and motivation must be plainly understood and constantly revisited.

The Deception of Self-Sufficiency

Finally, we must recognize the peril of independence in an endeavor that demands cooperation and interdependence. The book of Nehemiah demonstrates the value of team effort—not only as various families repaired different portions of the wall but also in the dividing of the numerous responsibilities (e.g., guarding). This Old Testament book also portrays the drawbacks of disunity. Chapter 5 recounts how the wealthy and the officials economically oppressed their own people for personal gain. Nehemiah admonishes them stating, "Each one of you is seizing the collateral from your own countrymen" (5:7). Such injustices led to an outcry from the people and questions concerning whether they would complete the building project.

The most amazing element in the book of Nehemiah is not that the cupbearer to an Assyrian king rebuilt a wall around an ancient Jewish city, but rather that this son of Hacaliah mobilized thousands of Jews to carry out this building assignment in the face of great adversity. Most likely the Jews experienced an array of emotions as Nehemiah informed them of his intentions. While some yelled, "Get going! Let's rebuild!" surely others questioned Nehemiah's sanity. Later, when the accusations were hurled, their lives were threatened, and the Jews were working from dawn to dusk, some of the Jews undoubtedly questioned the value of rebuilding. The text tells us of rifts between the people over grave issues including food and economic injustices (5:1–19). We also know that some Jews sided with the enemy and sought to derail Nehemiah's program (6:10–13). And yet, despite all of the circumstances surrounding the rebuilding of the walls, the Jews carried the project through.

Living with imperfect people creates frustration and discouragement. A good friend of mine used to halfheartedly joke, "Ministry would be great if it weren't for the people." Several years ago, I experienced this kind of frustration when I was involved with a singles ministry that never succeeded. Its demise was not due to a lack of support from the pastoral staff or from the married folk in the church undermining the program. Nor was it due to the amount of work required to bring the ministry to fruition. Instead, the problem was the single adults' inability to agree and function collectively. In a group of twenty singles, there were thirty opinions. A wall of commitment often crumbles under such stress fractures.

The Building Codes for Constructing a Wall

The above hindrances could have altered Nehemiah's building project, if not halted it altogether. And yet, this Jewish leader not only completed the wall in a timely fashion, but he also brought enormous reforms to the Jews living in Judah. In the process, Nehemiah demonstrated the importance of staying committed to the Lord, His work, and His people despite setbacks or hurdles. Nehemiah heeded several "building codes"—guidelines that reinforced his resolve and ensured the completion of his goal. These building codes are applicable to our own lives and guarantee spiritual success not only in our walk with the Lord but in our relationships with one another.

Commitment to the Lord

Even a cursory reading of the book reveals a man whose commitment to the Lord remained constant despite the circumstances of life. Nehemiah's secret lay not in his personality or some rare inner strength, but rather in an intimate relationship with his Lord. The opening prayer of the book displays the basis for this deep relationship. First, Nehemiah viewed God as transcendent, all-powerful, eternal, and holy. We witness this in Nehemiah's address: "O Lord God of heaven, great and awesome God, who keeps his loving covenant with those who love him and obey his commandments" (1:5). Second, Nehemiah also grasped the severity of his depravity. Before he begins to request God's assistance, Nehemiah states,

> I am confessing the sins of the Israelites that we have committed against you—both I myself and my family have sinned. We have behaved corruptly against you, not obeying the commandments, the statutes, and the judgments that you commanded your servant Moses. (1:6b–7)

This recognition of his own sin led Nehemiah to acknowledge his standing before God as a servant and his need for God's grace and power (1:6, 11). A proper understanding of God and himself led Nehemiah to a dependence upon and a longing for the Lord. This knowledge and an ongoing communion with Him are the foundation stones for commitment to the Lord. For when we grow in our relationship with the Lord and have experienced those intimate times, we realize not only our responsibility of devotion to the Lord but the wonderful privilege it is to serve Him.

There are no twelve easy steps or instant packets to obtain commitment to the Lord. Spiritual devotion requires sacrifice—sacrifice of self and all its desires. Prayer provides the venue for purifying our hearts, stripping our souls of self-centeredness and self-sufficiency, and molding our lives into the image of Christ. From the beginning of the book (1:5) until the end of the narrative (13:31), Nehemiah displays an intimate relationship with the Lord though his communication with Him. In fact, this book mentions prayer twelve times.[8] Bible scholar J. I. Packer writes,

> Nehemiah's walk with God was saturated with his praying, and praying of the truest and purest kind— namely, the sort of praying that is always seeking to clarify its own vision of who and what God is, and to celebrate his reality in constant adoration, and to rethink in his presence such needs and requests as one is bringing to him, so that the stating of them becomes a specifying of "hallowed be thy name . . . thy will be done . . . for thine is the kingdom, the power, and the glory."[9]

Nehemiah's commitment to the Lord rested not only on constant prayer, but also on knowledge of God's Word. An intimate relationship consists of communication flowing in both directions. Prayer allows us the opportunity to speak with the Lord, while the Scriptures provide a vehicle for God's communication to us. Chapter 9 shows that the Israelites stood from dawn to noon, listening to the reading of Moses' Law. So powerful was the Word of God that for days the people listened and responded in obedience. The Scriptures state that "all the people had been weeping when they heard the words of the law" (8:9b). As the Bible displays God's attributes and activities, it forces us to come to grips with our depravity, our need for Him, and our responsibility of commitment. Notice that immediately following the days of reading God's Word, the Levites recall who God is and what He has done in creation, the Abrahamic covenant, and the Exodus (9:5b–15). In so doing, the Levites focus upon the importance of complete devotion to the Lord. This value of God's Word can also be witnessed in the life of their leader. Nehemiah knew the Scriptures so well that he was able to do that which originated from the Lord. When Shemaiah delivered false prophecy, Nehemiah quickly recognized that God had not sent him (6:12).

As we observed earlier in this chapter, we often encounter obstacles in life that erode our commitments. Interestingly, when large or difficult events occur, I find that my commitment to the Lord initially appears strong. After all, it is easy to call on the Lord when I am unable to go any further or am incapable of the assignment. But when the project extends much longer than expected and opposition from various sectors begins to rise, I discover that my time with the Lord diminishes. When I left to study in Europe, I frequently went to the Lord in prayer and to read the Scriptures. There was no one else to turn to, no other resources to utilize. I was alone. However, as time passed, I grew weary with my studies, worried about my financial status, and missed family and friends back in the United States. Consequently, instead of walking more intimately with God, my time with the Lord waned. Ironically, I began to see Him as the One who had abandoned me. Commitment to the Lord is much easier when I am climbing a mountain than when I am down in the valley. Hence, I find Nehemiah's ongoing relationship with the Lord throughout this building project even more encouraging than his prayer prior to the undertaking.

Commitment in life must begin with devotion to the Lord—a devotion that is built on an intimate relationship with the Savior. The psalmist reminds us, "Unless the LORD builds the house, those who build it labor in vain" (Ps. 127:1 NRSV). Nehemiah models how to maintain commitment during life's laborious moments—times when devotion seems unattainable, or worse, undesirable. Nehemiah maintained an intimate relationship with his Lord through praying and studying the Bible. While the Scriptures never refer to Nehemiah as a "man who walked with God" or a "friend of God," his name does mean "the Lord comforts"—a meaning the narrative vividly portrays through his frequent communion with God.

Commitment to the Lord's Work

Nehemiah had an intimate relationship with the Lord, but he was also committed to the Lord's work. Pastor and theologian Gene Getz notes that Nehemiah "utilized all of the human resources available, including his intellectual capabilities, his human experiences, his accumulated wisdom, his role and position in life, and people with whom he came in contact."[10] And while we could spend time discussing what Getz and many other Christian and Jewish writers have observed concerning Nehemiah's leadership abilities, I would like to explore a more fundamental issue—why? Why would a cupbearer living hundreds of miles away from Jerusalem believe he could possibly accomplish such a task? Why would he have continued the project when the opposition escalated and tensions mounted between the Jewish people? Why commit yourself to a work that yields no personal profit? Why?

The answer begins with what we have just addressed—an intimate relationship with the Lord. Intimacy encompasses familiarity—knowledge of the other person's passions, thoughts, and actions. Why does a cupbearer take on the role of builder? Because he recognizes that God is leading him. When Artaxerxes grants provisions, Nehemiah states that "the good hand of my God was on me" (2:8). When Nehemiah arrives in Jerusalem, he acknowledges that "my God was putting on my heart to do for Jerusalem" (v. 12). When this soon-to-be contractor addresses the Jewish community, he indicates that God's hand is upon him (v. 18). And when Nehemiah calls for the Jews to assemble, he states, "My God placed it on my heart" (7:5). Men and women who have accomplished great things for the Lord are individuals whose affections rest upon the Lord and who are cognizant of His ways.

This attentiveness to God's leading results in peace and an assurance of His provision. Throughout the narrative we find Nehemiah trusting in the Lord. He prays to the Lord as he requests provisions from the Persian king (2:4). Likewise, when there was concern over safety, the Jews prayed and then stationed guards (4:9). In 6:9, Nehemiah calls for the Lord to strengthen his hands in the midst of foreign opposition. As he lives out the Lord's desires, Nehemiah can rest in the comfort of knowing that the Lord will act (2:20; 4:15). The "whys" dissipate when we know the Lord and that He has called us to tackle the assignment. No wonder Nehemiah could focus on his goals, plan thoroughly for their accomplishment, deal patiently and wisely with each problem as it arose, resist distractions, and refuse to be discouraged at any stage.[11]

We must also note that the intimacy Nehemiah possesses with his Lord yields a desire to serve. A final reason Nehemiah pursues this restoration project is for the privilege and joy of serving his beloved

Lord and allowing the Lord to use him. The opportunity Nehemiah had in service to the Persian king could not compare to the opportunity he had in working for the King of Kings. Nehemiah placed all of his gifts and abilities entirely at God's disposal. Herein lies a small but significant shift in the narrative. In Nehemiah's first prayer, he asks the Lord to remember the deeds of his servant Moses (1:8), but by the end of the book, Nehemiah asks the Lord to remember the deeds of Nehemiah (13:14, 22, 31; also, 5:19). One Bible scholar fittingly remarks, "Who would doubt that when [Nehemiah] entered the Lord's presence he heard the words, 'Well done, thou good and faithful servant?'"[12]

As believers, we too can live our lives according to the Lord's will and enablement. For we are "a chosen race, a royal priesthood, a holy nation, a people of his own" (1 Peter 2:9). As such, we can live successfully for Him because He guides (e.g., 2 Tim. 3:16–17), protects (e.g., 1 John 4:4), equips (e.g., Eph. 2:21–22), and ministers to us (e.g., 1 Cor. 2:12–16). Our service to the King must be steadfast and immovable (1 Cor. 15:58). In *Storms and Star*, Amy Carmichael, a single missionary to India, expresses the desire every believer should demonstrate as he or she does the Lord's bidding. Asking the Lord to deliver her from self-centeredness, she writes:

> *From prayer that asks that I may be*
> *Sheltered from winds that beat on Thee,*
> *From fearing when I should aspire,*
> *From faltering when I should climb higher,*
> *From silken self, O Captain, free*
> *Thy soldier who would follow Thee.*
>
> *From subtle love of softening things,*
> *From easy choices, weakenings—*
> *Not thus are spirits fortified;*
> *Not this way went the Crucified.*
> *From all that dims Thy Calvary,*
> *O Lamb of God, deliver me.*
>
> *Give me love that leads the way,*
> *The faith that nothing can dismay,*
> *The hope no disappointments tire,*

> *The passion that will burn like fire.*
> *Let me not sink to be a clod;*
> *Make me Thy fuel, Flame of God.*[13]

The "whys" can loom great and the obstacles will arise, but we must, like Nehemiah, be found faithful. In so doing our commitment to the Lord's work will remain strong and the Lord will be glorified (see Neh. 6:16). May we at the end of our lives be able to echo Paul's words in 2 Timothy 4:7: "I have competed well; I have finished the race; I have kept the faith!"

Commitment to One Another

The first-century Jewish historian Josephus closes his account of the life of Nehemiah with these words: "He was a man of kind and just nature and most anxious to serve his countrymen; and he left the walls of Jerusalem as his eternal monument."[14]

Not only was Nehemiah committed to the Lord and His words but also to His people. Chapter 5 presents one of the best examples of Nehemiah's service to his countrymen. Here we observe the Jewish governor refraining from collecting the food allotted to him and from purchasing land—an important commodity that ensured prosperity, security, and identity in an ancient civilization (5:14–17). In addition, he did not levy taxes for personal gain. One commentator writes, "In this respect Nehemiah set an example as a Persian official without precedent in the Persian empire as far as we know."[15] Typical Persian governors not only collected taxes for the central treasury but also additional funds for personal revenue.

Nehemiah lived out that which is commanded of all believers in the New Testament. The apostle John writes in 1 John 3:17–18, "But whoever has the world's possessions and sees his fellow Christian in need and shuts off his compassion against him, how can the love of God reside in such a person? Little children, let us not love with word or with tongue but in deed and truth." Here the Beloved Disciple reminds the believers in Asia Minor to share their material goods and property. In so doing, they would demonstrate God's love. In fact, the question, "How can the love of God reside in such a person?" can be read as a declarative statement—"The love of God cannot possibly reside in this person." John calls the believers to not just provide lip service but to allow the truth to produce godly activity.

I may be wrong, but I often get the impression from TV sitcoms or even from some of my friends that singles are selfish with their resources. And yet, surprisingly, George Barna reports, "Married people . . . give away only half as much of their income as singles donate to churches and other nonprofit organizations. In fact, the average widowed adult donates three times more of his or her income to causes than the married couples. Relatively few single adults are wealthy, but they tend to donate a greater slice of their pie to those in need than do married couples."[16] This data encourages me. Of course, singles must remember that we are not comparing ourselves to married individuals but attempting to align ourselves with God's Word. All that we have belongs to the Lord. May we serve as good stewards of all that He has given to us.

Because Nehemiah understood the value of community, he gave sacrificially to his people. This Jewish leader wisely recognized that no one person could have completed the restoration of Jerusalem's walls and gates. Nehemiah needed the approval, provision, and protection of Artaxerxes; the endorsement of the local Jewish officials; and the cooperation of the Israelites if the wall restoration was to take place.

This importance of interrelationships is also accentuated in the local church. Despite our independent American mind-set, we are part of a community of believers. In *Whatever Happened to Commitment?* Edward Dayton reminds us that Christians are to love one another (John 13:34; 15:12; 1 Peter 4:8), forgive one another (Eph. 4:32), care for one another (1 Peter 4:10; John 13:14), teach one another (Gal. 5:13), be subject to one another (1 Peter 5:5; Eph. 5:21), be hospitable to one another (1 Peter 4:9), honor one another (Rom. 12:10), and confess to one another (James 5:16).[17] In Wendy Widder's *A Match Made in Heaven: How Singles and the Church Can Live Happily Ever After*, she properly writes,

> While it is true that only in Christ can we find meaning in our personal lives, such meaning can only be fully understood as we also discover the joy of belonging to each other in a dynamic, transforming way. We are

> living stones because of the Living Stone, and we are
> joined to the rest of the building. The Christian life is
> about interdependence, not independence. We must
> be in this together—growing, sharpening, helping,
> challenging—or we're not really in it at all.[18]

The older I grow in this state of singleness, the more independent I become. With that independence comes a self-sufficiency that can border on selfishness. People and their needs can become my inconveniences and the thought of "group work" makes my stomach churn. Recently I was asked to serve on a committee, and since "no" is absent from my vocabulary, I agreed. Big mistake! Hours were wasted as I listened to members pontificate about various matters of business. The "pool of ignorance" seemed only to confirm my disdain for cooperative endeavors. Unfortunately, such experiences, my ever-growing independence, and my strong "type A" personality fight against my recognition of the importance of the body of Christ and the need to support one another. The book of Nehemiah graphically illustrates the value of the community of God's people working together to accomplish the work of the Lord.

Did Nehemiah have the right to collect an income from the people? Yes. Were there times when he was sick of the people's complaints and ungodly behavior? Probably. Out of frustration, could he have left the community of Jews and returned to Artarxerxes' palace? Yes. However, this man who walked with God recognized not only the importance of loving the Lord your God with all your heart, soul, and mind, but also of loving your neighbor as yourself (Lev. 19:18; Luke 10:27).

Conclusion

The book of Nehemiah demonstrates that commitment is costly. It requires our time, our resources, our thought life, and even our very soul. The depth of these requirements will increase with every obstacle we encounter. While Nehemiah served as one of the greatest general contractors in Israel's history, his commitment to the Lord, His work, and His people met stones of ridicule, potential cracks of depression, a dangerous clouding of his vision, and the possible deception of independence or self-sufficiency. However, this cup-bearer willingly paid the costs necessary to ensure that his commitments stood strong. Underlying the edifice of commitment to the Lord, he possessed an intimate relationship with his God. Nehemiah's commitment to the Lord's work rested upon foundation stones of the recognition of the Lord's calling and enablement, as well as his dependence on Him. And finally, we observed that an emphasis upon service and a value of community held together Nehemiah's commitment to the Jews. May we, like Nehemiah, be able to ask the Lord to remember us for good as we faithfully live out our commitment.

For Reflection

1. Why do you think most Christians fail to do a great work for God (e.g., lack of direction, lack of giftedness, simple laziness, apathy)? Explain.
2. Read through the book of Amos and make a list of the lifestyle changes God challenges the religious leaders to make so they will care for people the way God does.
3. Think of an area of life where you have been bogged down or ineffective. Journal about how you can trust God for that area, and make a plan of action to overcome it. Share your plan with a good friend.
4. To what extent are you involved in your local church? Are you doing your part by utilizing your talents, abilities, personal resources, and gift of singleness?
5. What worthy projects do you have in process that are only half finished—and at a standstill? Select the one that will be the most spiritually productive for others in your life. Decide now that you are going to complete that project as soon as possible.

8

John the Baptist

Always a Groomsman, Never a Groom

> Your singleness . . . can be achieving for you an eternal glory that is going to far outweigh all the things that you think you missed out on.
>
> —Elisabeth Elliot
> (widow of missionary martyr Jim Elliot, speaker, and author
> of *Through the Gates of Splendor* and *Passion and Purity*)

Recently one of my former students asked if I would play the piano for her wedding. As I struggled to respond, I was grateful she could not read my mind. Otherwise, she would have certainly thought I was schizophrenic. On the one hand, I consider participating in someone's wedding a great honor and a delight. On the other hand, the prospect of playing for yet another wedding is like caring for a sick cat, donating my wisdom teeth, or joining a group of junior highers for a two-week camping trip. While it is a joy to witness firsthand the union of two people I know and love, weddings often bring to the surface feelings of inadequacy, jealousy, bitterness, and loneliness. To make matters more difficult, I have not survived a wedding where someone did not ask me when I am getting married. (If I had a dollar for every time I've heard that question, I could purchase a villa in Tuscany!) Perhaps this is why I keep telling my parents that the next wedding I play for better be my own or the marriage feast in Revelation 19.

"Always a bridesmaid but never a bride" plagues many single adults who have lost count of the number of times they have participated in a wedding. In the gospels we meet an individual who is constantly serving as a groomsman of sorts. Content with his role, this single man constantly seeks ways to elevate the "man of the hour." This radical individual is John the Baptist. In John 3:26, the disciples of John ask, "Rabbi, the one who was with you on the other side of the Jordan River, about whom you testified—see, he is baptizing, and everyone is flocking to him!" John replies:

> No one can receive anything unless it has been given to him from heaven. You yourselves can testify that I said, "I am not the Christ," but rather, "I have been sent before him." The one who has the bride is the bridegroom. The friend of the bridegroom, who stands by and listens for him, rejoices greatly when he hears the bridegroom's voice. This then is my joy, and it is complete. He must become more important while I become less important. (vv. 27–30)

John the Baptist provides the perfect conclusion to our journey toward a biblical perspective on singleness. His life models Paul's words in 1 Corinthians 7; and in many ways, the baptizer summarizes the messages of each of the other biblical people we have studied. John's recognition of life's purpose and its true blessings furnish him with the necessary qualities to be an effective instrument for the cause of Christ. Let us explore how these two areas allow John the Baptist to live victoriously.

Recognizing the True Purpose of Life

No bystander wonders why a group of people in tuxedos and fancy dresses is standing on the steps of a church near a curbside limousine on a Saturday morning. In the same way, a life lived effectively for the Lord is unmistakable. It is marked by a proper understanding of our calling and our role in this world. John demonstrates both aspects of a purpose-filled life.

A Proper Understanding of Our Calling

John the Baptist clearly understood his directive for life. The baptizer knew who sent him and he knew the purpose for his existence. When the Jewish leaders interrogated John about his identity, John replied, "I am the voice of one shouting in the wilderness, 'Make straight the way for the Lord'" (1:23). John clearly recognized that his role, which consisted of heralding in the messianic age, did not come from some church body or self-proclamation. Rather, John's ministry originated with God (John 1:6). Furthermore, neither John's piety nor his talents warranted this selection. In fact, the Old Testament foretold of one who would prepare the way for the Messiah (see Isa. 40:3; Mal. 3:1). And later in Luke 1, we find the angel Gabriel proclaiming to the elderly priest Zechariah that he and his wife would give birth to a son—a son whose name would be John (v. 13). Our friend of the Bridegroom did not stumble into his messianic role. Neither did John happen to possess the right physique or IQ. John served in this unique position simply because the Lord chose him.

We must recognize that God has also called all those who know Jesus Christ as their personal Savior. As stated by John the Baptist, "No one can receive anything unless it has been given to him from heaven" (3:27). In other words, no one can come to Jesus unless the Father has so willed it (see John 6:37). Elsewhere in the New Testament, we read that God "chose us in Christ before the foundation of the world" (Eph. 1:4). Paul continues by stating that the reason for the Lord's selection of us was merely for His pleasure (vv. 5, 9). As witnessed in the life of John and previously in the prophet Jeremiah (chap. 4), before our parents began thinking of having us, our heavenly Father selected us for Himself.

In the midst of living single, when questions of identity, self-worth, and the future arise, we must not forget that the Lord of Lords, the God of the Universe, called us. Questions of Who is there for me? or Who cares to know me intimately? can haunt the soul. We must cling to the truth that He chose us long before we ever thought of Him. His calling lay not in necessity, because I am the last single adult available, or out of pity because I am single; but rather, God selected me because He loved me. His affection makes gratuitous any action on my part; and if I accept His gift of love—His Son's death, burial, and resurrection for the forgiveness of my sins—I am

His child. Paul proclaims to the churches in Galatia, "And because you are sons, God sent the Spirit of his Son into our hearts, who calls 'Abba! Father!' So you are no longer a slave but a son, and if you are a son, then you are also an heir through God" (Gal. 4:6–7).[1] The truth that the Father loves me and that I am His son indicates that I can do nothing to earn or forfeit that love. I already have it. When I struggle with the absence of a "better half," I need to submerse myself in His love. Bathe in it. Swim in it. Soak in it.

God's calling provides the basis, the support, and the direction for a life with true meaning and purpose.

A Proper Understanding of Our Role

Serving as the best man in a wedding entails numerous tasks—from organizing the bachelor's party to providing a toast at the wedding reception. At the heart of these responsibilities lies support for the groom. Whether this means encouraging, comforting, or warming cold feet, the best man directs 100 percent of his attention to the groom. I have never known a best man who tried to steal the show at a wedding. After all, the special day centers only on two people—the soon-to-be-married couple.

Similarly, in first-century Palestine, the friend of the bridegroom sought to support the newly married couple. The exact role John the Baptist refers to in John 3:29 is unclear. As pointed out by Johannine scholar Raymond Brown, "Some think of the best man as at the bride's house, standing guard and waiting to hear the noise of the groom's procession as it comes to fetch the bride. Others picture the best man as at the groom's house after the bride has been brought there; he rejoices to hear the groom speaking with the bride."[2] Whatever his exact responsibilities, we do know that the best man served as the agent for the groom in arranging the marriage and he played an important part in the wedding festivities. John recognized that he was not the Christ (1:20), and his disciples were witness to his denial (3:28). Jesus came from above, but John was from the earth (3:31).

The baptizer denies he is the Christ and indicates that the Christ is the One "who is coming after me. I am not worthy to untie the strap of his sandal!" (1:27). Untying sandal straps was so debasing that a Jewish slave or disciple was exempt from performing this service (see *b. Qiddushin* 22b; *b. Ketubbot* 96a). John does not consider himself worthy to do even this menial job for the Messiah. So significant are John's words that Paul cites them in his sermon at the synagogue in Pisidian Antioch (Acts 13:25). John understands that all that he is and all he does stems from God's grace. He also recognizes that his life must serve to glorify Christ—not himself. The baptizer's own words summarize his position best: "He must become more important while I become less important" (John 3:30). One New Testament scholar comments concerning these words:

> This is John's swansong, his last word in the gospel. It is also the formula under which every statement about John stands. His witness abides (5:32–6; 10:40–2), but John slips off the stage. His death is not even mentioned, so unimportant is his person.[3]

As believers, we have been called to serve as friends of the Bridegroom. Jesus declares, "If anyone wants to become my follower, he must deny himself, take up his cross, and follow me. For whoever wants to save his life will lose it, but whoever loses his life for my sake and for the gospel will save it" (Mark 8:34–35). In my opinion, the greatest difficulty of Jesus' words is not in taking up the cross. I realize the implications of crucifixion—the pain, humiliation, and ultimately death—but the first command, denying oneself, serves as the greatest hurdle. I believe that I would struggle far less dying for my beliefs than daily sacrificing my life with all its hopes and dreams. And yet this is precisely what Jesus did for us when He came to earth in the form of a servant (Phil. 2) and hung on a tree. The Savior willingly submitted to the Father's will. I love the words penned by Oswald Chambers: "The call of God is not the echo of my nature; my affinities and personal temperament are not considered. As long as I consider my personal temperament and think about what I am fitted for, I shall never hear the call of God."[4] John the Baptist forwent a spouse, a family, and even his disciples for the cause of Jesus Christ.

Occasionally, I hear inaccurate statements concerning the Savior's code of discipleship. A common theory proposes that singleness is one's act of denying and of bearing a cross. This understanding of Jesus's command is seriously flawed. First, as we concluded in our discussion of Paul's words in 1 Corinthians 7, singleness is a gift from God and should never be relegated to the realm of punishment, discipline, or shame. Second, taking up a cross does not mean we carry burdens or have problems; it simply means that all that I have, all that I am, and all that I could have belongs to the Lord. My life is for His glory as I share in His shame and death. In other words, "to take up the cross means to identify with Christ in His rejection, shame, suffering, and death."[5] Dietrich Bonhoeffer, an unmarried German pastor who was executed by the Nazi party in 1945, wrote in his must-read *The Cost of Discipleship:*

> To deny oneself is to be aware only of Christ and no more of self, to see only him who goes before and no more the road which is too hard for us. Once more, all that self-denial can say is: "He leads the way, keep close to him."[6]

Summary

A life of purpose concerns itself not with power, prestige, or possessions. Neither does a purposeful life require a spouse and 2.5 children. Rather the purpose of life encompasses what the Lord has done and the actions He expects if we respond to His calling. John the Baptist was ever aware of the undeserved grace he received. The Baptizer possessed a unique calling, and with that selection came special tasks. As noted above, the Lord has called each believer. As a result, each child of God has been given the assignment of following after Him. After all, life's true purpose or "chief aim," according to the Westminster Catechism, is to glorify the Lord.

Recognizing the True Blessings of Life

Humanly speaking, many might classify John the Baptist's life as worthless. He led a nomadic life, exhibited eccentric behavior, maintained an unusual diet, wore odd apparel, and delivered an offensive message. In addition, his ministry robbed John of the pleasures of growing up in Jerusalem and serving in the temple with his father, Zechariah. Ultimately, his service to God resulted in having his neck severed by Herod Antipas. And yet, John's investment by living a life with purpose yielded dividends no money market or stock option could match.

Blessings Bestowed Through Us

John the Baptist had the opportunity to be used by the Lord. Both in the promise of John's birth and in Zechariah's song of praise, Luke highlights that John functioned as a prophet. First, the angel declared that John would be filled with the Spirit, implying a prophetic inspiration (1:15; cf. Isa. 61:1; Ezek. 11:5; Joel 2:28). Second, Zechariah called his son "the prophet of the Most High" (Luke 1:76). Third, the tasks assigned to John in Luke 1 resemble those of a prophetic office (cf. 2 Chron. 15:1–4). The angel specifically stated, "He will turn many of the people of Israel to the Lord their God. And he will go as forerunner before the Lord in the spirit and power of Elijah, to turn the hearts of the fathers back to their children and the disobedient to the wisdom of the just, to make ready for the Lord a people prepared for him" (Luke 1:16–17). Later Zechariah prophesied, "You will go before the Lord to prepare his ways, to give his people knowledge of salvation through the forgiveness of their sins" (vv. 76–77). John the Baptist had the unique privilege of serving as the eschatological prophet Elijah who heralds the news of the arrival of God's salvation.[7] Even from his mother's womb, we can observe John's role as a messianic forerunner. Luke informs us that John "leaped" in his mother's womb in the presence of Mary (1:41–44). The Greek verb for "leap," *skitra*, can be used as an expression of joy at eschatological salvation (cf. Ps. 114:4, 6; Mal. 4:2). Based upon the strong allusion to Malachi 3 elsewhere in Luke's first two chapters, the evangelist recalls the promise of Malachi that the coming of the Lord would give great joy. No wonder Jesus declared John to be "the greatest born among women" (see Matt. 11:11–15).[8] The baptizer derived his greatness and honor from his unique role of preparing the way for the Messiah.

John the Baptist vividly demonstrates in word and deed that our service to others stems from God's gracious hand. Great men and women of the faith—such as John Calvin, John Knox, Jonathan Edwards, Dwight Moody, and Mary Slessor—left their imprints on human history. Each person was aware of his or her own special work, possessing different talents, upbringing, education, and experiences.

And yet they had nothing that did not originate from heaven via the direct appointment and decree of God. While John the Baptist was unmarried, performed no miracles (John 10:41), and surely was unimpressive in his presentation (Matt. 11:7–8), the Lord used him mightily. We must be careful not to base our value to the Lord's work on our marital status, giftedness, or appearance. As F. B. Meyer writes, "Use what thou hast. The five barley loaves and two small fishes will so increase, so they are distributed, that they will supply the want of thousands. Do not dare to envy one more successful and used than thyself, lest thou be convicted of murmuring against the appointment of the Lord."[9]

God's calling upon our lives, the gift of His Son, and the indwelling of the Holy Spirit warrant our service. We are His and we have the privilege and obligation of allowing Him to use us for His glory. The apostle Paul spends the first eleven chapters of the book of Romans discussing the doctrine of justification. He reminds the believers that they need to be declared righteous, what justification entails, and how it affects their lives. After penning these words, the apostle then spends the second half of this epistle discussing natural responses of those who are justified. He begins, "I exhort you, brothers and sisters, by the mercies of God, to present your bodies as a sacrifice—alive, holy, and pleasing to God—which is your reasonable service" (Rom. 12:1). Such an exhortation is far from outlandish or overbearing. As Paul correctly notes, it is "reasonable." And while Paul reminds believers of their obligation to the Lord, he also highlights in the latter part of Romans the privilege of building up our brothers and sisters in Christ (12:3–21), showing Christ to the world (13:1–10), extending Christ's love to one another (13:11–14:23), and helping individuals in Christ's name (15:1–13).

I constantly marvel that the Lord should use me. One only needs to follow me around for a day and understand my struggles to see why I say this. Seldom a day passes when I do not wonder why the Lord allows me to teach His precious Word. How thankful I am to know that "in Christ God was reconciling the world to himself, *not counting people's trespasses against them,* and he has given us the message of reconciliation. Therefore we are ambassadors for Christ, as though God were making His plea through us. We plead with you on Christ's behalf, 'Be reconciled to God!'" (2 Cor. 5:19–20, emphasis mine). Paul addresses how he has been reconciled and is a representative of that reconciliation. One commentator notes that Paul's wording "insists that when he speaks the *kerygma* [gospel] God himself is the chief actor and it is his voice that men and women hear and his authority that is brought to bear upon people's lives."[10] We have the privilege of sharing the blessing that we have experienced in our own lives. What wonder that He should not count our sin! What wonder that He should allow us to serve Him! And what wonder that He should allow us to carry His message!

We must acknowledge that having the opportunity to serve as a conduit of God's blessing mandates faithfulness. John the Baptist was eventually imprisoned because of his preaching against Herod Antipas's immorality. As he awaited possible capital punishment, John reflected on his ministry, particularly his relationship with Jesus of Nazareth. He sent his disciples to ask Jesus, "Are you the one who is to come, or should we look for another?" (Luke 7:19). While John undoubtedly became discouraged and disillusioned, I am astounded at his perseverance. Instead of resigning from the messianic forerunner office or relinquishing his prophetic license, the baptizer acknowledges that he will keep on searching if Jesus is not the Coming One.

In the early 1930s, Dietrich Bonhoeffer left his German pastorate and fled to England to pastor a German-speaking parish there. Several months later, however, he returned to his home country, primarily because of a letter penned by the world-renowned theologian Karl Barth. Encouraging Bonhoeffer to fulfill his duty to Germany, Barth wrote the following words:

> What is all this about "going away," and "quietness of pastoral work," etc., at a moment when you are wanted in Germany? You, who know as well as I do that the opposition in Berlin and the opposition of the church in Germany as a whole stands inwardly on such weak feet! . . . I think that I can see from your letter that you, like all of us—yes, all of us!—are suffering under the quite common difficulty of taking "certain steps" in the present chaos. . . . One simply cannot become weary now. Still less can one

go to England! . . . You must now leave go of all these intellectual flourishes and special considerations, however interesting they may be, and think of only one thing, that you are a German, that the house of your church is on fire, that you know enough to be able to help and that you must return to your post by the next ship.[11]

The privilege of loving others for the sake of Christ demands perseverance of believers. May we utilize the gifts God has granted us—yes, even singleness—for His glory! In so doing, we will experience firsthand the blessings He will bestow on others through us.

Blessings Bestowed on Us

Despite my reluctance to participate in weddings, I eventually agreed to play for my former student's "special" day. I was so thankful I did. I always forget what a blessing it is to witness and take part in these monumental events. While "denying oneself" and "taking up a cross" might suggest the absence of any joy, a person who yields to the Lord's calling and displays His glory will not only be a blessing to others, but will also be personally blessed. Notice how in John 3:29 the Baptizer indicates that his joy is complete when he fulfills his role as the friend of the Bridegroom. John's joy resides in the opportunity to prepare hearts for the coming of the Messiah, to behold the One generations had longed to see, to witness firsthand the coming of the Spirit as a dove and to hear the voice of the Father, and to baptize the Messiah and usher in His ministry.

True personal satisfaction in life is found in recognizing what the Lord has done for us. He should use us, and we should be busy serving Him. The apostle Paul frequently refers to joy in his epistle to the Philippians.[12] Interestingly, the term never refers to Paul's own comforts or pleasures. Rather, the source of Paul's joy lies in the preaching of Christ, in the believers and their spiritual growth, and in the opportunity to serve the Lord. Taking up our cross and following Him does not exempt us from hardship, but it will bring true joy. As the title of the old hymn correctly notes, "There Is Joy in Serving Jesus."[13]

Anyone who knows me recognizes my limited athletic ability.

I am one of the few boys who grew up a Hoosier yet cannot play basketball. It is a scary thing to observe. During seminary, a group of guys always met during the week to shoot hoops. On occasion, I would tag along for a short time—not to play, of course, but only to chat or watch. One afternoon, a couple of the guys asked if I would be willing to join them. Despite reminders of my inability to dribble, let alone shoot, they persisted. While I suspect that Michael Jordan played better than I do by the time he was four, I was very grateful that my friends asked me to be part of their game. On a much grander scale, the thought that we can play a part in God's sovereign, perfectly orchestrated plan for humanity should make us ecstatic. The idea that the Father would use us to share the good news concerning His Son should fill us with joy. As so eloquently penned in Romans 11:33, who can explain or explore the depths and the riches of our Lord's mercy?!

Personal blessings to those who enlist in the Lord's service reside not only in the here and now but also in the future. The apostle Paul writes in 1 Corinthians 3, "Each builder's work will be plainly seen, for the Day will make it clear, because it will be revealed by fire. And the fire will test what kind of work each has done. If what someone has built survives, he will receive a reward" (vv. 13–14). Most rewards and blessings will be granted after death, not before. Paul understood this: "For our momentary, light suffering is producing for us an eternal weight of glory far beyond all comparison because we are not looking at what can be seen but at what cannot be seen. For what can be seen is temporary, but what cannot be seen is eternal" (2 Cor. 4:17–18). Elsewhere, we read that the Lord promises a crown of life to those who love Him (James 1:12). And in 2 Timothy 4:8, we are reminded that those who long for the Lord's appearing will obtain a crown of righteousness.

It would be a sad day if we appeared before the One who called us before the creation of space and time and lavished His love upon us, and were told we had squandered His grace and mercy. This embarrassment would be coupled with the regret of realizing all the blessings we forfeited in order to live life for ourselves. Imagine what John the Baptist would have missed had he not been obedient! Not only would he have forfeited his right to prepare the way for the Messiah, but he would have missed out on hearing "well done, thou good and faithful servant." If we live for the "here and now," we will miss out in the "then and there."

We can also note from 1 Corinthians 3:13–14 that future rewards are dependent upon quality rather than quantity. The Lord will judge us on the kind of work we accomplish, not the magnitude of the assignment. In other words, there will be a different grading scale for each person. I applaud the following words by Charles Swindoll in *Improving Your Serve:*

> We humans are impressed with size and volume and noise and numbers. It is easy to forget that God's eye is always on motive, authenticity, the real truth beneath the surface, never the external splash. . . . The dear older lady who prays will be rewarded as much as the evangelist who preaches to thousands. The quiet friend who assists another in need will be rewarded as much as the strong natural leader whose gifts are more visible.[14]

We are not rewarded because of the way He created us, but rather on how we allow Him to use what He gave us. We do not have to be a prophet like John the Baptist. Thankfully, we will probably never be asked to wear a leather girdle and eat locust. But we have been called to serve the Lord. In so doing, we will not only experience the blessing of watching the Lord use us in the lives of others, but we will also reap the joy of serving Him and the rewards that await us.

Finally, there lies ahead the ultimate future reward for each believer. We, the church, will be united with our Groom, Jesus Christ. The apostle Paul highlights this event in his words to the believers at Corinth: "For I am jealous for you with godly jealousy, because I promised you in marriage to one husband, to present you as a pure virgin to Christ" (2 Cor. 11:2). While we may have spent many weekends in this life serving as bridesmaids or groomsmen and wishing for our own weddings, there will be a day when we will stand in the center with our Beloved. Anne R. Cousin's "The Sands of Time Are Sinking" says it well:

Oh! I am my Beloved's, and my Beloved's mine!
He brings a poor, vile sinner into His house of wine;
I stand upon His merit, I know no other stand,
Not e'en where glory dwelleth in Immanuel's land.

The bride eyes not her garment, but her dear bridegroom's face;
I will not gaze at glory, but on my King of grace;
Not at the crown He giveth, but on His pierced hand;
The Lamb is all the glory of Immanuel's land.[15]

Conclusion

Recent studies show that "fewer than five out of every one hundred single adults in America are absolutely committed to the Christian faith, are actively seeking to grow in each of the pillar areas of spirituality, regularly invest themselves in intentional spiritual growth efforts and can identify and give evidence of using their spiritual gifts to serve God and His people."[16] We need single and even married adults who possess, as John the Baptist, a compelling motivation to abandon the world and devote themselves to the things of God. John understood and remained focused upon his calling despite the hardships, sacrifices, and persecution. John's appointment from the Lord spurred him on to living out the responsibilities set before him.

The baptizer's life also displays the blessings that come from a life of purpose. The individual who is willing to give his life away will glean more than the world could possibly grant or afford. John experienced the privilege of serving the Lord as the messianic forerunner. In addition, the baptizer bore the honor of not only preparing hearts for the coming of the Messiah but introducing those around him to the Savior.

For Reflection

1. Following Christ is costly. In what areas might a person struggle that would prevent that individual from becoming a devoted follower of Christ? While we normally think of negative areas (e.g., besetting sins), could there be areas that are amoral and

even inherently good but hinder one's commitment to following Jesus? What might one of these areas be?

2. What are you facing that is hindering or could potentially hinder you from having a life totally yielded to Jesus Christ?

3. Missionary Karen Watson was gunned down in Iraq while attempting to provide humanitarian relief in the name of Jesus. In explaining her rationale for going to this dangerous location, she wrote: "To obey was my objective, to suffer was expected, his glory my reward." Based upon our study of John the Baptist, what does it take for someone such as Karen Watson to display such devotion? Is her commitment to Christ possible for every believer?

Conclusion

As we have journeyed through the lives of various singles in the Bible, we have noted that the single life is not only a viable option but it also affords us the opportunity to live for the Lord—undistracted by particular concerns of this world. This godly perspective on the single life is what allowed Paul to travel over thousands of miles preaching the gospel, Anna to minister despite her social inadequacies, Jeremiah to cope with loneliness, Ruth to move beyond shattered dreams, Joseph to withstand temptation, Nehemiah to remain committed, and John to serve in the midst of adversity. We have but one life to live for the Lord. Our calling flows from the Lord's gracious hand, warrants our obedience, and accepts no excuses.

We have also noted that the Lord honors those who use their "gift" for His glory. Reflect upon the various biblical personalities we have encountered. The obedience of Paul results in the gospel spreading to the Gentiles; Anna serves as one of the two witnesses needed to validate the ministry of Jesus; Mary, in contrast to Martha, provides the perfect model of loving the Lord; Jeremiah spurs many on to faithfulness and truth; Ruth becomes the grandmother of King David; Joseph delivers his people from a great famine; Nehemiah restores the capital city of the Jews; and John the Baptist heralds the messianic age. In addition, we observed that a life of purpose serves not only as a conduit of blessings to others, but leads to personal blessings. These blessings both equate with joy in this present life and foreshadow the rewards that are ours in the future. Of course, the greatest blessing comes when we appear before our Groom and have the privilege of resting in His presence.

Serving God single? These eight biblical characters demonstrate not only that this is possible but that immense blessings can accompany such devotion. In keeping with Paul's exhortation in 1 Corinthians 7, these portraits reveal that it matters not whether we are married or single, but that we are obedient. These individuals understood the true meaning of life. It concerns not a spouse, an education, or a lucrative job. Rather, a life worth living remains faithful to His calling, follows the Lord despite the costs, and presses forward to the prize. As we stand in the midst of such a great cloud of witnesses, may our lives reflect John the Baptist's mission: "The Lord must become more important while I become less important!"

Endnotes

Chapter 1—Paul: The "Gift" of Singleness

1. Anthony C. Thiselton, *The First Epistle to the Corinthians*, New International Greek Testament Commentary (Grand Rapids: Eerdmans, 2000), 16–17.

2. At one point, Corinth—with a population of approximately 300,000 citizens and 460,000 slaves—had at least twelve temples with over 1,000 temple prostitutes (Robin Barber, *Greece*, Blue Guide, 5th ed. [New York: Norton, 1987], 261). The city's reputation was so corrupt that Corinth was a byword of excess and sexual license.

3. The Corinthians were declaring that "it was good for a man not to have sexual relations with a woman" (1 Cor. 7:1).

4. Romans 1:11; 5:15–16; 6:23; 11:29; 12:6; 1 Corinthians 1:7; 12:4, 9, 28, 30–31; 2 Corinthians 1:11; 1 Timothy 4:14; 2 Timothy 1:6; 1 Peter 4:10.

5. Paige Benton, "Singled Out by God for Good," *Regeneration Quarterly* 3 (1997): 21.

6. Robert Gundry notes in his commentary on Matthew's gospel: "Nothing in the context favors understanding the passage in terms of freedom from marital cares for the sake of evangelistic endeavor, or because of an eschatological crisis, or for considerations of ceremonial purity or asceticism. . . . Understanding self-imposed eunuchism as abstinence from remarriage makes largely irrelevant the usual references to 1 Cor. 7:7, 25–40" (*Matthew*, 2d ed. [Grand Rapids: Eerdmans, 1994], 382–83). The immediate text supports Jesus' prohibiting divorce with remarriage and remains silent on the matter of contentment. The text, however, does portray the single life of Christian men as an act of discipleship.

7. The word for "control" speaks of keeping impulses or deep desires in check. For instance, the word occurs in Genesis when Joseph holds back his tears upon seeing his brothers (Gen. 43:31 Septuagint [LXX]).

8. David Garland, "The Christian's Posture Toward Marriage and Celibacy: 1 Corinthians 7," *Review and Expositor*, 77 (1980): 357.

9. Winston Churchill's oft quoted comment about Russia was first made in a radio address October 1, 1939. Then First Lord of the Admiralty, he was speaking about the Soviet-German Treaty of Friendship, signed September 29.

10. We must be careful when discerning God's will not to allow the barometer of desire to determine God's leading. Neither should we expect a subjective confirmation, ignore the context of biblical promises, or strip God's will of reason.

11. Kimberly Hartke, "Singular Hope," *Leadership Journal*, (Spring 2002): 52.

12. Gerald F. Hawthorne, *Philippians*, Word Biblical Commentary, vol. 43 (Waco: Word, 1983), 43:198.

13. Philip Yancey, *Reaching for the Invisible God* (Grand Rapids: Zondervan, 2000), 284.
14. "Survey Question Responses," Purposeful Singleness, Inc. at singleness.org/question/7-02.shtml.
15. A rabbi at the end of the second century said of the life pattern of a Jewish boy, "At five years old he comes to the reading of the Scripture, at ten to the Mishnah [rabbinic literature], at thirteen, to the practice of the commandments, at fifteen to the Talmud [rabbinic literature], at eighteen to marriage . . . " (*m. Avot* 5:21).
16. The likelihood that Paul had been previously married provides further credence to his comments (see John McRay, *Paul: His Life and Teaching*, [Grand Rapids: Baker, 2003], 33–37). The apostle has then experienced both "gifts." He knew firsthand the advantages of the single life.
17. Anthony C. Thiselton notes that the key word, *amerimnos* ("free from anxiety"), is rare in the New Testament, "but occurs in Seneca as an attribute of celibacy which offers care-free concentration in contemplative philosophy" (*First Epistle to the Corinthians*, 586). The word can be found in the teaching of Jesus to indicate a single-mindedness rooted in God (cf. Matt. 6:25, 28; 10:19).
18. Will Deming, *Paul on Marriage and Celibacy*, Society for New Testament Studies Monograph Series 83 (Cambridge: Cambridge University Press, 1995), 177–97. Emphasis added. Deming is quick to note that Paul is not stressing the imminence of the End or any heavenly existence. Paul's omission of the coming of the Lord seems to support Deming's view.
19. Anthony C. Thiselton citing Benjamin Witherington in *First Epistle to the Corinthians*, 582.
20. Ibid., 583.
21. John Calvin, *First Epistle of Paul the Apostle to the Corinthians*, trans. J. W. Fraser (Grand Rapids: Eerdmans, 1960), 160.
22. Lucien Legrand, *The Biblical Doctrine of Virginity* (New York: Sheed and Ward, 1963), 98.
23. George Barna, *Single Focus* (Ventura, Calif.: Regal, 2003), 88.
24. E. Earle Ellis identifies nine designations Paul uses of his coworkers: brother, apostle, minister, fellow slave, partner, toiler, fellow soldier, fellow prisoner, and coworker ("Coworkers, Paul and His," in *Dictionary of Paul and His Letters*, ed. G. F. Hawthorne, R. P. Martin, and D. G. Reid [Downers Grove, Ill.: InterVarsity, 1993], 183–89).
25. F. F. Bruce, *The Pauline Circle* (Grand Rapids: Eerdmans, 1985), 8–9.
26. D. Edmond Hiebert, *In Paul's Shadow* (Greenville, S.C.: Bob Jones University Press, 1973), 102. For further discussion on the relationship between Paul and Timothy, see Charles R. Swindoll's *A Man of Grace and Grit: Paul* (Waco, Tex.: Word, 2002), 315–30.
27. William E. Phipps, "Paul's Attitude Toward Sexual Relations," *New Testament Studies* 28 (1982): 129.
28. "Survey Question Responses," Purposeful Singleness, Inc. http://www.singleness.org/question/10-01.shtml.
29. Thiselton, *First Epistle to the Corinthians*, 592.

Chapter 2—Anna: Left at the Altar

1. *Ecclesiasticus* or *Sirach* 42.14.
2. See, e.g., *De opificio mundi* 151–52 and *Quaestiones in Genesim* 1:33.
3. *Testament of Reuben*, 5.
4. James Jeffers, *The Greco-Roman World of the New Testament Era* (Downers Grove, Ill.: InterVarsity, 1999), 249.
5. David E. Holwerda, "Widow," in *International Standard Bible Encyclopedia*, ed. G. W. Bromiley, 4 vols. (Grand Rapids: Eerdmans, 1979–1988), 4:1060.
6. The phrase "until eighty-four years" is ambiguous and could refer to Anna's age rather than the period of her widowhood. As noted by Darrell Bock, "The most direct impression is that her widowhood was eighty-four years long, since widowhood is

the subject of the sentence" (*Luke 1:1–9:50*, Baker Exegetical Commentary on the New Testament [Grand Rapids: Baker, 1994], 252).

7. Tamala M. Edwards, "Flying Solo," *Time*, (28 August 2000): 50.

8. Cf. *b. Megillah* 14a. Philip the evangelist's four daughters are also noted for this position within God's community (Acts 21:8–9).

9. While a parallel between these two women does exist, this does not deny the historicity of Luke's account (cf. J. K. Elliott, "Anna's Age (Luke 2:36–37)," *Novum Testamentum* 30, no. 2 [1988]: 100–102; and I. Howard Marshall, *The Gospel of Luke*, New International Greek Testament Commentary [Grand Rapids: Eerdmans, 1978], 124).

10. Richard Bauckham, *Gospel Women: Studies of the Named Women in the Gospels* (Grand Rapids: Eerdmans, 2002), 101.

11. Marshall, *The Gospel of Luke*, 123.

12. For further discussion, see Bauckham, *Gospel Women*, 94–95.

13. For further discussion, see Gordon D. Fee, *1 and 2 Timothy, Titus*, New International Biblical Commentary on the New Testament (Peabody, Mass.: Hendrickson, 1988), 80–81.

14. *M. Rosh HaShanah* 1:8.

15. Bauckham, *Gospel Women*, 77.

16. Ibid., 98.

17. Ibid., 98–101.

18. "Giving back praise" also occurs in Daniel 4:37 when Nebuchadnezzar thanks God for the restoration of his health.

19. Charles R. Swindoll, *Hope Again* (Dallas: Word, 1996), 146.

Chapter 3—Martha: Living Life in the Fast Lane

1. George Barna, *Single Focus* (Ventura, Calif.: Regal, 2003), 26.

2. A third-century A.D. Jewish writing states that many rabbis were against any instruction for women (cf. *m. Sotah* 3:4; also, cf. Josephus *Against Apion* 2:201).

3. R. C. Sproul, *The Holiness of God* (Wheaton, Ill.: Tyndale, 1988), 141.

4. Warren Wiersbe, *God Isn't in a Hurry* (Grand Rapids: Baker, 1994), 10.

5. "Nothing Between" written by Charles A. Tindley. Public domain.

6. According to Leviticus 25, the Israelites were to declare every fiftieth year a jubilee year. During this time liberty was granted to Israelites who were in bondage to any of their countrymen, ancestral possessions were to be returned to those who had been compelled to sell them because of poverty, and the land was to remain fallow.

7. William Still, preface to *Rhythms of Rest and Work* (n.p., n.d.).

8. Richard A. Swenson, *The Overload Syndrome* (Colorado Springs: NavPress, 1998), 181–90.

9. Leonardo da Vinci, *Notebooks*, vol. I. Quoted at enthinkexist.com/quotation/every_now_and_then_go_away-have_a_little/14052.

10. William Wilberforce, quoted in E. M. Bounds, *Power Through Prayer*, chapter 19.

11. Luke 3:21; 5:15–16; 6:12; 9:18–22, 28–29; 10:17–21; 11:1; 22:39–46; 23:34.

12. "Casting" is a participle of means.

Chapter 4—Jeremiah: All Alone in a Couple's World

1. Robert S. Weiss, *Loneliness: The Experience of Emotional and Social Isolation* (Cambridge, Mass.: MIT Press, 1973), cited by Leigh Devereaux in "Loneliness," eeducationamerica.com, 1.

2. Recent statistics seem to indicate that loneliness among Americans will only rise. Between 1960 and 1995, single-person households rose from 13 to 25 percent of the total, while households of married couples with children dropped from 44 to 25 percent, according to the U.S. Census Bureau. In addition, census projections suggest that the number of people living alone will increase 8.4 percent between 2000 and 2010 (Laura Pappano, *The Connection Gap: Why Americans Feel So Alone* [London: Rutgers University Press, 2001], 152).

3. J. Schonwald, "NIA Will Fund Study About Loneliness: Its Physical Risks," *The University of Chicago Chronicle* 21, no. 5 (November 15, 2001): 1.
4. He was a native of Anathoth (Jer. 1:1), a village three miles northeast of Jerusalem. Jeremiah was descended from the priest Abiathar, who was banished to Anathoth by Solomon for committing treason. Abiathar had supported Solomon's son, Adonijah, in an attempted coup (1 Kings 2:26–27). The descendants of the other chief priest, Zadok, were thus in charge of the temple until the exile.
5. J. R. Soza, "Jeremiah," in *New Dictionary of Biblical Theology*, ed. B. S. Rosner, D. A. Carson, and G. Goldsworthy (Downers Grove, Ill.: Intervarsity, 2000), 224.
6. Terence E. Fretheim, *Jeremiah*, Smyth and Helwys Bible Commentary, ed. R. S. Nash (Macon, Ga.: Smyth and Helwys, 2002), 247.
7. G. von Rad, "The Confessions of Jeremiah," in *A Prophet to the Nations: Essays in Jeremiah Studies* (Winona Lake, Ind.: Eisenbrauns, 1994), 346.
8. J. R. R. Tolkien, *The Fellowship of the Ring* (Boston: Houghton Mifflin, 1965), 70.
9. Eugene H. Peterson, *Run with the Horses: The Quest for Life at Its Best* (Downers Grove, Ill.: InterVarsity, 1983), 37.
10. C. S. Lewis, *The Problem of Pain* (New York: Macmillan, 1943), 41.
11. Fretheim, *Jeremiah*, 239.
12. Similar cries unto the Lord can be found in Psalm 102 and Job 19.
13. A. Heschel, *The Prophets* (New York: Harper, 1962), 138.
14. Warren Wiersbe, *Lonely People* (Lincoln, Neb.: Back to the Bible, 1983), 79.
15. Karl Barth, *Epistle to the Romans* (London: Oxford University Press, 1952), 183.
16. Peterson, *Run with the Horses*, 108.
17. R. E. O. White, *The Indomitable Prophet: A Biographical Commentary on Jeremiah* (Grand Rapids: Eerdmans, 1992), 161.
18. Pappano, *The Connection Gap*, 47.
19. Cited by E. Watke Jr., *The Problem of Loneliness* (Augusta, Ga.: Revival in the Home Ministries, 2001), 3.

Chapter 5—Ruth: Encountering Shattered Dreams

1. Robert L. Hubbard Jr., *The Book of Ruth*, New International Commentary on the Old Testament (Grand Rapids: Eerdmans, 1988), 95.
2. For further discussion on this unique phrase, see K. Nielsen, *Ruth*, Old Testament Library (Louisville: Westminster John Knox, 1997), 46–47; and Hubbard, *The Book of Ruth*, 102–3.
3. While drunk, Lot had sexual relations with his daughters, the result of which was the birth of Moab and Ammon (Gen. 19:30–38).
4. The Hebrew word for "cling," *dabaq*, connotes firm loyalty and deep affection. The word is used in Genesis 2:24 to speak of a man who leaves his parents to "cling" to or "unite" with his wife.
5. Katherine Doob Sakenfeld, "Naomi's Cry: Reflections on Ruth 1:20–21," in *A God So Near: Essays on Old Testament Theology in Honor of Patrick D. Miller*, ed. B. A. Strawn and N. R. Bowen (Winona Lake, Ind.: Eisenbrauns, 2003), 137.
6. Hubbard, *The Book of Ruth*, 74.
7. Ben Patterson, *Waiting: Finding Hope When God Seems Silent* (Downers Grove, Ill.: InterVarsity, 1989), 102.
8. Katherine Doob Sakenfeld, *Ruth*, Interpretation (Louisville: John Knox, 1999), 33.
9. Nielsen, *Ruth*, 50.
10. I. J. Gelb, "The Ancient Mesopotamian Ration System," *Journal of Near Eastern Studies* 24 (1965): 231, 236.
11. Also noted by Hubbard, *The Book of Ruth*, 179.
12. Warren Wiersbe, *Be Committed* (Wheaton, Ill.: Victor Books, 1993), 33.
13. The word is also used to describe Boaz in 2:1.
14. Often attributed to Edison, but the original source is apparently lost. See, for example, quotes.worldvillage.com/i/b/Thomas_Edison.

15. J. H. Sammis, "Trust and Obey."

16. Robert L. Hubbard Jr. eloquently states, "The book offers no awesome display of divine might, no terrifying glimpse of the divine being. Only the words of main characters keep alive an awesome awareness of God's presence at all" (*The Book of Ruth*, 69).

17. A kinsman-redeemer's main tasks were to restore ownership of alienated clan property through redemption, to free fellow clansmen from poverty-induced slavery (Lev. 25:25–30, 47–55; Jer. 32:1–15), and avenge the killing of a relative (cf. Num. 35:12, 19–27). Boaz's marriage to Ruth should not be confused with a levirate obligation. This was legally binding on the widow as on the deceased's brother. A kinsman-redeemer functioned not as a means to provide an heir for the deceased but to provide for the security and protection of the widow. Ruth was looking for a "redeemer"—one who would marry her for the purpose of protection and support, not the provision of an heir for the deceased. Naomi's instructions in Ruth 3:1–4 and Ruth's words to Boaz (3:9) calling for the sole removal of the destitution and disgrace of Ruth's widowhood support this understanding of Boaz's role in the narrative.

18. William Cowper, "God Moves in a Mysterious Way." Public domain. Taken from *The Handbook to the Lutheran Hymnal* (St. Louis: Concordia, 1941): 358.

19. Joni Eareckson Tada, "Thriving with Limitations: When Life Hasn't Met Your Expectations How Can You Minister to Others?" *Leadership* 17, no. 3 (1996): 62.

20. Sakenfeld, "Naomi's Cry," 143.

21. Hubbard, *The Book of Ruth*, 261.

22. Frederick Bush, *Ruth, Esther,* Word Biblical Commentary (Dallas: Word, 1996), 55.

Chapter 6—Joseph: Purity in the Midst of Temptation

1. *Our Daily Bread*, October 2, 1992.

2. George Barna, *Single Focus* (Ventura, Calif.: Regal, 2003), 64.

3. Jewish literature written around the first century A.D. hails Joseph's actions in Genesis 39 as a model for all people to follow (Josephus, *Jewish Antiquities* 2.42–43; *Jubilees* 39.3–8; *t. Reu.* 4:8–9; and Philo, *On Joseph*, 9.40).

4. J. C. O'Neill, "Temptation," in *The Westminster Dictionary of Christian Theology*, ed. A. Richardson and J. Bowden (Philadelphia: Westminster, 1983), 562.

5. Richard Exley, *Deliver Me* (Nashville: Nelson, 1998), 6.

6. It is important to remember that temptation, in and of itself, is not sin. Only when one yields to its beckoning call has temptation become sin. James writes, "Let no one say when he is tempted, 'I am tempted by God,' for God cannot be tempted by evil, and he himself tempts no one. But each one is tempted when he is lured and enticed by his own desires" (1:13–14).

7. Cornelius Plantinga Jr., preface to *Not the Way It's Supposed to Be: A Breviary of Sin* (Grand Rapids: Eerdmans, 1995), xii–xiii.

8. Potiphar not placing Joseph in charge of "the bread which he did eat" probably refers to personal matters (see V. P. Hamilton, *The Book of Genesis: Chapters 18–50*, New International Commentary on the Old Testament [Grand Rapids: Eerdmans, 1995], 460).

9. Such an understanding of lions can be observed throughout the Old Testament. In Psalm 17, David describes his enemies as "a lion eager to tear, like a young lion lurking in ambush" (v. 12 NRSV). For further examples, see Jeremiah 49:19; 50:44; and Lamentations 3:10.

10. Interestingly, the Greek words for "discipline" (*nephw*) and "to be alert" (*gregorew*) are used primarily in eschatological contexts (cf. Matt. 24–25; Mark 14; 1 Thess. 5; 1 Peter 4:7). The danger is real and sudden.

11. John Owen, *Sin and Temptation: The Challenge of Personal Godliness,* ed. J. H. Houston (Minneapolis: Bethany House, 1996), 120.

12. Charles Swindoll, *Joseph: A Man of Integrity and Forgiveness* (Dallas: Word, 1998), 34.

13. F. B. Meyer, *Joseph: Beloved—Hated—Exalted* (Fort Washington, Penn.: Christian Literature Crusade, n.d.), 30.

14. Joshua Levinson also adds that "for Joseph, to be seduced by Potiphar's wife, to give in to his own desires, is to lose not only the defining characteristic of maleness itself, but also his cultural identity" ("An-Other Woman: Joseph and Potiphar's Wife Staging the Body Politic," *The Jewish Quarterly Review* 87, nos. 3–4 [1997]: 294).
15. Hamilton, *The Book of Genesis,* 469.
16. John Walton, *Genesis NIV Application Commentary* (Grand Rapids: Zondervan, 2001), 671.
17. According to the Law, convicted rapists were executed when both parties were free citizens (see Deut. 22:23–27). A Hebrew slave touching his Egyptian master's wife would certainly expect no better fate (cf. Gordon Wenham, *Genesis 16–50,* Word Biblical Commentary, vol. 2 [Dallas: Word, 1994], 377).
18. James Montgomery Boice, *Genesis Volume 3: Living by Faith, Genesis 37–50* (Grand Rapids: Baker, 1987), 923.
19. Plantinga, *Not the Way It's Supposed to Be,* 12.
20. David Wells, *No Place for Truth, or Whatever Happened to Evangelical Theology* (Grand Rapids: Eerdmans, 1993), 183.
21. First-century Jewish historian Josephus extols the patriarch's understanding of the danger of sin, noting that Joseph would rather "suffer unjustly and endure the severest penalty, rather than take advantage of the moment by an indulgence of which he was conscious that he would justly deserve to die" (Josephus, *Jewish Antiquities* 2.51).
22. Plantinga, *Not the Way It's Supposed to Be,* 80.
23. Jürgen Moltmann, *Theology of Hope* (New York: Harper and Row, 1975), 22.
24. Owen, *Sin and Temptation,* 45–48.
25. Barna, *Single Focus,* 54.
26. Ibid., 53.
27. Ibid., 70.
28. Hamilton, *The Book of Genesis,* 459.
29. George Lawson, *The Life of Joseph* (1807; reprint, Carlisle, Pa.: Banner of Truth Trust, 1988), 45.
30. Aleksandr Solzhenitsyn, *The Gulag Archipelago: 1918–1956: An Experiment in Literary Investigation* (New York: HarperCollins, 1992), 3.5.5:615.

Chapter 7—Nehemiah: Not Going "A-Wall" (AWOL)

1. See P. E. Becker and H. Hofmeister, "Work, Family, and Religious Involvement for Men and Women," *Journal for the Scientific Study of Religion* 40 (2001): 707–22.
2. George Barna, *Single Focus* (Ventura, Calif.: Regal, 2003), 56.
3. Whether Nehemiah was a eunuch has been debated (Edwin M. Yamauchi, *Persia and the Bible* [Grand Rapids: Baker, 1991], 260–64); however, Persian kings normally used eunuchs (cf. 2 Kings 20:18; Esth. 1:10) as the cupbearer would have frequent contact with the queen.
4. Ibid., 259–60.
5. Nehemiah's project would in particular hamper the influence of Sanballat, probably the governor of Samaria; Geshem, the leader of a powerful block of Arab communities; and Tobiah, the governor of Ammon.
6. Josephus, *Antiquities* 11.174–76.
7. Donald Campbell, *Nehemiah: Man in Charge* (Wheaton, Ill.: Victor Books, 1979), 21.
8. Nehemiah 2:4; 4:4–5, 9; 5:19; 6:9, 14; 9:5–37; 13:14, 22, 29, 31.
9. J. I. Packer, *A Passion for Faithfulness: Wisdom from the Book of Nehemiah* (Wheaton, Ill.: Crossway Books, 1995), 44–45.
10. Gene Getz, *Nehemiah: A Man of Prayer and Persistence* (Ventura, Calif.: Regal Books, 1981), 27.
11. Packer, *A Passion for Faithfulness,* 66–67.
12. Campbell, *Nehemiah,* 119.

13. Amy Carmichael, "Prayer." From *Mountain Breezes* by Amy Carmichael. Copyright © 1999 The Dohnavur Fellowship. Published by CLC Publications. Used by permission.
14. Josephus, *Jewish Antiquities* 11:183.
15. F. C. Fensham, *The Books of Ezra and Nehemiah* (Grand Rapids: Eerdmans, 1982), 198–99.
16. Barna, *Single Focus*, 36.
17. Edward Dayton, *Whatever Happened to Commitment?* (Grand Rapids: Zondervan, 1984), 156.
18. Wendy Widder, *A Match Made in Heaven: How Singles and the Church Can Live Happily Ever After* (Grand Rapids: Kregel, 2003), 127–28.

Chapter 8—John the Baptist: Always a Groomsman, Never a Groom

1. Similarly Moses reminds the Israelites: "We were Pharaoh's slaves in Egypt, but the Lord brought us out of Egypt in a powerful way" (Deut. 6:21).
2. Raymond Brown, *The Gospel According to John I–XII*, Anchor Bible, vol. 29 (Garden City: Doubleday, 1979), 152.
3. Walter Wink, *John the Baptist in the Gospel Tradition*, Society for New Testament Studies Monograph Series 7 (Cambridge: Cambridge, 1968), 95.
4. Oswald Chambers, *My Utmost for His Highest* (New York: Dodd, Mead, and Co., 1935), 16.
5. Warren Wiersbe, "A Time to Be Renewed," *Christianity Today* 32, no. 5 (1988): 26.
6. Dietrich Bonhoeffer, *The Cost of Discipleship* (New York: Touchstone, 1995), 88.
7. Malachi 4:5–6 predicts the coming of Elijah who would prepare the way for YHWH. Many first-century Jews) messianic forerunner or some type of eschatological figure (cf. John 1:19–28).
8. J. A. Fitzmyer points out that "born of women" is an Old Testament expression for "pertinence to the human race" (*The Gospel According to Luke (I–IX)*, Anchor Bible, ed. W. F. Albright and D. N. Freedman, vol. 28 [Garden City: Doubleday and Co., 1981], 675; also, cf. 1QS 11:21; 13:14; Gal. 4:4; and *Gospel of Thomas* 46a).
9. F. B. Meyer, *John the Baptist* (Grand Rapids: Zondervan, 1934), 93.
10. Ralph P. Martin, *The Worship of God: Some Theological, Pastoral, and Practical Reflections* (Grand Rapids: Eerdmans, 1982), 105.
11. Quoted by Mark Galli in "Karl Barth," *Christian History* 19, no. 1 (2000): 25.
12. The word *joy* occurs in Philippians 1:4, 25; 2:2; 4:1; while the word "rejoice" appears in 1:18; 2:17–18; 3:1; 4:4, 10.
13. Words by O. J. Smith, copyright 1931, renewal in 1959 with Rodeheaver Company.
14. Charles Swindoll, *Improving Your Serve* (Dallas: Word, 1996), 195–96.
15. Anne Cousin, "The Sands of Time Are Sinking," from a poem based on the letters of Samuel Rutherford (1600–1661). First published in 1857.
16. George Barna, *Single Focus* (Ventura, Calif.: Regal, 2003), 84.

Scripture Index